A Woman's Way

to Incredible Success in Business

Inspirational Advice and Real-Life Lessons
from 20 Prominent Businesswomen

Mary-Ellen Drummond

Adams Media Corporation
Holbrook, Massachusetts

Published by

Adams Media Corporation

260 Center Street, Holbrook, MA 02343

www.adamsmedia.com

ISBN: 1-58062-520-7

Printed in Canada.

J I H G F E D C B A

Library of Congress Cataloging-in-Publication Data
Drummond, Mary-Ellen.
A woman's way to success in business : inspirational
advice and real-life lessons from 20 prominent
businesswomen / Mary-Ellen Drummond.
p.   cm.
ISBN 1-58062-520-7
1. Businesswomen--United States.
2. Success in business--United States. I. Title.
HD6095 .D78   2001
650.1'082--dc21   00-065008

This book is available at quantity discounts for bulk purchases.
For information, call 1-800-872-5627.

Contents

Acknowledgments

Heartfelt thanks and standing ovations to the following people because, without their hard work, support, and inspiration, this book would not have been possible.

John Drummond, my husband, and my daughter, Erica, lovingly and consistently provided me with a daily dose of inspiration.

Gaylene Pringle, my friend and colleague, gave her enthusiastic support and encouragement, which helped to launch and sustain this project. It was over lunch at Gaylene's house that the idea for this book was born.

Nancy Hancock Williams, a former client, longtime friend, and professional colleague, was an ongoing source of wisdom, savvy business advice, and unending assistance. Nancy helped with the original book proposal and generously provided editing guidance and expertise along the way.

Karen O'Connor, friend and professional speaking colleague, also provided her professional writing and editing assistance with the book proposal. She served as an adviser and sounding board throughout the writing and compilation process.

Mo Rafael, a longtime friend from my early days at North Coast Toastmasters, provided her thorough and thoughtful skills to editing the entire manuscript of *A Woman's Way to Incredible Success in Business*. I marveled at her attention to detail, careful eye, outstanding organizational skills, and ability to see the big picture.

Betsy Mill, professionally known as BZ Betsy, kept very busy being the best word processor I've ever known. She worked diligently to meet and exceed all deadlines and kept the authors' contributions organized and safe. Without her, I would not have had a finished manuscript.

James Alvord, attorney, provided prompt, courteous, and professional counsel whenever needed.

Karen Winston, my publicist and marketing director for Polished Presentations International, is greatly esteemed for her visionary thinking and ongoing creativity.

Barbara Doyen, my literary agent, became my agent for several reasons, the most important one being that I liked her as a person. She's honest, she's real, and she does what she says she's going to do. In addition to all that, she's persistent, hard-working, and always positive. Her ongoing enthusiasm for this book was a tremendous source of energy.

My editors, Elizabeth Gilbert and Jere Calmes at Adams Media Corporation deserve acknowledgment for the way they energetically embraced this project and saw the value and potential impact of *A Woman's Way to Incredible Success in Business*.

And a huge amount of gratitude to all of the contributing authors of this compilation for their time, talents, and contributions.

Marie Betts-Johnson
Jeanette S. Cates, Ph.D.
Peggy Eddy, CFP
Janet Lapp, R.N., Ph.D.
Florence Littauer, Ph.D.
Pam Lontos
Eileen McDargh
Nanci McGraw
Mary Marcdante
Karen O'Connor
Diane Parente
Gaylene Pringle
Lorna Riley
Judi Sheppard Missett
Nancy Smith
Sondra Thiederman, Ph.D.
Jacqueline Townsend Konstanturos
Julie White, Ph.D.
Nancy Hancock Williams, MBA

Thank you, thank you, one and all!

Foreword

From technology to the trades, from fitness to finance, from politics to public speaking—women are changing the face of American business and culture in subtle as well as obvious ways. Perhaps our most important contribution is the re-creation of success itself. Throughout the pages of *A Woman's Way*, this re-creation is evident. Mary-Ellen Drummond has brought together a group of dynamic contributing authors and role models whose personal stories and real-life examples form the heart of this book.

Each of the authors of the 21 chapters is recognized in her chosen field of professional speaking, financial planning, sales, fitness, training, technology, spirituality, and more. Most are self-starting entrepreneurs who have created their own businesses. Whether self-employed or employed by others, each one is an example of personal and professional success in every sense of the word.

As you benefit from their experience and expertise, you'll find yourself inspired to choose your own path to success. Each chapter will equip you to seize new possibilities, and to dream, define, and determine your own future in business and in life.

While reading this book, keep a highlighter in hand. Mark the pages, take notes, and set goals for yourself as you review the ideas, techniques, and action steps in each chapter. The authors' combined wisdom, advice, and real-life lessons will provide the tools and motivation needed to succeed in the competitive climate of the information age.

Our new century promises to be the most exciting time in history for women in business, as people reach for success at an accelerated pace. As more doors open and more opportunities become available, I believe that *A Woman's Way to Incredible Success in Business* will help all women redefine their own future and the future of business in America.

> Dr. Marjorie Blanchard,
> Co-Founder and Director,
> Office of the Future
> The Ken Blanchard Companies,
> Escondido, CA

Introduction

Over the years, I've come to realize that no one can know all there is to know about success in business, and no one can make it alone in today's world. In order to attain our dreams and goals—in business and in life—we need to surround ourselves with positive, supportive, and like-minded achievers who are willing to help us.

To reach my goals, I learned the importance of finding outstanding role models for what I wanted to learn, accomplish, and become. And, to my delight, I found them. Through networking opportunities in professional organizations, at conventions, conferences, associations, and social gatherings, I met dozens of women who were living their dreams as professional business owners, entrepreneurs, educators, speakers, and authors—far more than I had ever imagined. I was not only inspired to "reach for the stars" in my own business, but I was also motivated to help showcase the success of others so that the cycle of achievement could be passed on to as many other women as possible.

When I began thinking about creating *A Woman's Way to Incredible Success in Business*, theoretically, it seemed that it would be a relatively easy task to invite women I knew, respected, and admired to write a chapter on their particular area of business expertise. In retrospect, more than two years after the idea struck me, I find myself shaking my head and saying, "Easy? What was I thinking?" I knew then, as I know now, that any worthwhile achievement is not easy. Just like success, it requires time, thought, study, hard work, passion, persistence, and the help of other people.

A Woman's Way to Incredible Success in Business was a collective, collaborative process that involved many people, many skills, and many months to make it all come together. The authors who contributed to this book are active businesswomen of achievement who gave not only their time, but also their stories, inspiration, and expertise because they share the belief that no one can make it alone in business today. They know that we are capable of soaring to greater heights when we share our ideas, skills, techniques, and visions to help one another make good things happen.

I believe that any woman can benefit from reading this book if—and it's a big "if"—she is motivated to change. Change is not easy, but with the specific ideas and examples given in this book, combined with desire and hard work on her part, she can achieve the success she dreams of and deserves. And, as every woman succeeds, I hope that she, in turn, will inspire and help others by her example and by serving as their mentor. Together we can make a dramatic difference in the world of business and in life.

The impact of women in business is growing from coast to coast. In May 1999, the *Los Angeles Times* reported the latest figures from the National Foundation for Women Business Owners: There were "9.1 million women-owned firms nationwide representing nearly one in four U.S. businesses . . . a 103% increase from 1987." The NFWBO also revealed that "women-owned firms now generate more than $3.6 billion in annual sales, up more that 436% from 1987." In California, women own more than 1.2 million enterprises representing nearly 40 percent of all companies in the state, and New York has about 600,000 women-owned businesses.

Too often, women are overly modest regarding personal achievements. We discount our successes and our power. Therefore, more than ever, as increasing numbers of women seek success in business, it is vital that they have role models, mentors, and examples of what is truly possible. That is what I hope you will find in the pages of *A Woman's Way to Incredible Success in Business*. I want this book to open your eyes, your mind, and your heart to the unlimited possibilities for achievement in the new millennium, and I hope that you will discover for yourself how you, too, can experience incredible success!

Mary-Ellen Drummond
Rancho Santa Fe, California

chapter one

Passion Is the Key!

JUDI SHEPPARD MISSETT
Founder and Chief Executive Officer, Jazzercise, Inc.

To be truly successful in any endeavor, it must engage your passion.

Passion propels you—it keeps you focused, pushes you to work your very hardest, commits you to excellence, fuels your belief in yourself, and sustains you during difficult times.

How many times have you heard, or had, a great business idea, only to see it remain just that, an idea? Ideas become actions when passion is in play. Just think of the business success stories you've read in which entrepreneurs defied the odds, simply because they had an overwhelming enthusiasm for their vision.

If you're passionate about what you do, it becomes an integral part of your life—like breathing. Mark Twain once said, "When one can make his work his own, it becomes play." For me, that's the whole idea! When you love what you do, you find amazing ways to accomplish your objectives. You're not afraid to pursue every avenue and take risks to realize success.

When I began teaching Jazzercise classes, "aerobic" exercise had not yet reached the masses. Still, dancing was my great love, and I had an exceptional desire to make it accessible to a wider audience. So, my idea of turning students away from the mirrors, simplifying routines, and focusing on fitness rather than traditional technique and performance meshed perfectly with the growing public interest in exercise during the 1970s. But getting from that point of origin to a multimillion-dollar, international franchise organization involved creativity and a willingness to adapt to the current business climate.

My personal policy is never to be constrained by what is traditional or "acceptable." When I began teaching classes at community recreation facilities, I took my daughter Shanna with me. She played quietly in the back, or danced on her own up front, while I led more than 100 women through a 45-minute workout. Not your typical child-care arrangement, but it worked. The point I'm trying to make is that I was willing to operate from the basis of my own expectations, not those of others, which left me the freedom to find ways to accomplish my goals.

> When you love what you do, you will find amazing ways to accomplish your objectives.
>
> —Judi Sheppard Missett

A similar example can be found in the way I first marketed my business. As a one-woman show with no office or support staff, I didn't have the resources to create and purchase traditional advertising to raise awareness of the Jazzercise program. Instead, I posted flyers in public places, relied on and encouraged word-of-mouth referrals, rounded up students, performed demos at community events, and submitted news releases to the local media about anything and everything I was doing in regard to the program. Although some of these areas were new and not immediately comfortable for me, my passion for the program itself prompted me to go out on a limb and give them a try.

Adapting to an Ever-Changing Business Environment

As in any business, our customer base is always evolving. Whether we're attracting new customers or addressing the changing needs of our loyal student base, at Jazzercise we are always looking forward to what's new and what's next.

This is an elementary rule in business today, but one that can easily be overlooked. The truth is, organizations often fight change. It is risky to tamper with what initially created your success, but it's an even greater risk to remain static.

> If you're passionate about what you do, it becomes an integral part of your life—like breathing.
>
> —*Judi Sheppard Missett*

The trick is to stay focused on your core purpose or mission. For Jazzercise, that is to bring fitness to individuals in communities worldwide through a quality program of dance exercise. To help our franchisees stay focused on our common goal, we've clarified this mission in a "Jazzercise Vision 2000" statement that reads: *People participate in Jazzercise in every community worldwide every day. Dynamic instructors teach well-attended classes and make a positive impact on people's lives.*

Personally, I stay in touch with this goal by continuing to choreograph all our new exercise routines (every 10 to 12 weeks) and teach classes every week at our Jazzercise Center in Oceanside, California. Still, as a corporation, we are free to introduce new programs, to restructure management, to change our training, to do whatever is necessary to continue to accomplish our mission year after year.

When I first began teaching Jazzercise, the classes consisted of a 45-minute combination of standing and floor routines, the first of which raised our heart rates for at least 30 minutes and the latter of which toned and stretched our muscles. There was no extra equipment, no special attire.

If you walk into a Jazzercise class today, you'll see a variety of equipment, from weights to steps to resistance tubes and balls. You'll notice a variance in class length, from 30 minutes to 90 minutes depending on the workout. And, you'll be struck by the fashionable and functional shoes and clothing worn by students and instructors alike.

The exciting thing is that these changes—many of which came in anticipation of or response to student requests—brought additional opportunity to the business at large. Only a few years after Jazzercise began, we launched a successful fitness merchandise mail-order division called Jazzertogs. Our various class formats, which offer a variety of class lengths and use a range of equipment, have given instructors the opportunity to market to new audiences and get their foot in the door at new facilities. A case in point is our "Cardio Quick" 30-minute aerobic workout, which has allowed many Jazzercise instructors to start on-site classes at corporations during the noon hour.

Over the years we've experienced many changes in the way we train and support our instructors as well. By 1977, I was still a one-woman operation, teaching 20 to 25 classes a week, losing my voice, taxing my body, and sacrificing time with my family. A friend casually suggested that I train some instructors to help teach the classes. Although the thought of turning my "baby" over to others and maintaining the same quality and energy was frightening, I knew the program could not continue growing if I didn't do something different. So I picked five women who were participating in my classes and who had some dance background, and a new age of instructor training and certification was born.

> My personal policy is never to be constrained by what is traditional or "acceptable."
>
> —Judi Sheppard Missett

In two short years we went from group sessions in my backyard to videotaping routines for distribution to instructors in other states. We took a chance on the new technology of camcorders and VCRs, and it paid off well. Instructors moving from Southern California were able to take the program with them to new communities across the country and the world. Today, Jazzercise has a division called JM DigitalWorks that offers full video production and duplication services to Jazzercise and more than 350 outside clients.

By 1980, our practice of contracting with independent instructors also was no longer adequate, and we officially became a franchise company, enabling thousands of individuals—the vast majority of whom are women—to successfully launch their own businesses.

Although each of the examples just noted obviously worked to our advantage, we've had our share of setbacks, too. No company can accurately predict the whims of the public or the trends in the marketplace 100 percent of the time. However, a willingness to try and to learn from our mistakes has placed us—and can place you—well in front of the pack. Change is growth, and the bottom line is that it can make a huge difference in the productivity and profit of your company.

> The truth is organizations often fight change. It's risky to tamper with what initially created your success, but it's an even greater risk to remain static . . . the trick is to stay focused on your core purpose or mission.
>
> —*Judi Sheppard Missett*

Listen to Your Customers and Employees

Your customers' needs and desires are your opportunities! The examples I just gave are evidence. When students wanted quality exercise clothing bearing the Jazzercise name, a fitness merchandise division was born. When video equipment made it possible for instructors to take Jazzercise to distant locations, the program grew. It's that simple.

Your customers and employees are a wonderful resource for new ideas, so I advocate cultivating an atmosphere where suggestions are encouraged and discussed. Likewise, I recommend hiring quality people and trusting them to make decisions on your behalf. I have never been a whiz at figures or finance, so I place my trust in someone who is. I have high expectations regarding employee performance, but I've found that the confidence I place in others inevitably translates into confidence in themselves. At Jazzercise, we create an environment of energy and enthusiasm that is open to creative ideas and that allows individuals the opportunity to be both responsible and accountable.

I'm also a strong believer in being open and responsive to people's capabilities, not just their past experience. I've gambled on many individuals whose enthusiasm, energy, and passion proved to be much more valuable to Jazzercise than their previous work experience may have indicated.

Maintain a Balance— Both Professionally and Personally

In any job, whether you're the CEO or secretary, there are tasks you love and tasks you dread. To be successful, you must exercise discipline to meet *all* your responsibilities. For instance, my first love is dance, so my favorite tasks still involve choreography, teaching, screening music, etc. If I chose to, I could make that a full-time job. But that would spell disaster for my business. Although I don't enjoy finances as much and am more than willing to hire a sharp staff to take charge, I must still be aware of the trends and projections and be prepared to make educated decisions based on their guidance.

The same holds true for Jazzercise franchisees. Many come from a dance or fitness background and have less interest in the "business" of Jazzercise. I remind them regularly to split their time equally between teaching and marketing. Although offering students a great workout is paramount to attracting and maintaining customers, it is not enough. They need to be actively involved in all aspects of their business, whether it's designing and executing a marketing plan, tracking student attendance and receipts, or negotiating rent with facility directors and landlords.

Striking a balance between your personal and professional life is just as essential. Personally, I don't "do lunch" and I don't attend business dinners and cocktail parties. Those times of the day are precious to me, and I dedicate them to myself and my family. I also feel very strongly about getting involved with philanthropic causes. Over the years, Jazzercise has raised more than $23 million for a wide variety of charities. Helping others in need is a wonderful way to keep things in perspective.

Pay Attention to Your Instincts

Having the appropriate information is vital in any business decision, but once you have it at your disposal, don't ignore your gut reaction. I also refer to this as my "little voice." Rarely has it let me down, if I've listened to it. My little voice is the voice of truth. I've learned that when you are passionate about something, your instincts will not lead you astray.

> If you can dream it, you can do it! Winners are never surprised when they win.
>
> —*Judi Sheppard Missett*

My instincts have also molded my philosophy for doing business. And over the years I've had the opportunity to observe how a strong commitment to this philosophy has served to make Jazzercise the success it is. I articulate this philosophy as four basic principles.

Commit to Your Principles

First, I conduct my business with sensitivity, fairness, and caring. Personal relationships build businesses, whether you're dealing with customers, employees, or colleagues, so I insist on acting with honesty, integrity, and responsibility in all business dealings.

Second, I always think big. My personal credo is: "If you can dream it, you can do it!" Jazzercise's appearance in the Opening Ceremonies of the 1984 Summer Olympics in Los Angeles is my favorite example of this phenomenon. We surprised many naysayers when our persistence and belief in what we could offer led to a dance number that featured several hundred Jazzercise instructors and was televised around the world.

Third, create excitement! There's no better way to attract people to your cause than to spark their enthusiasm. People are drawn to fun projects, products, services, and/or organizations. Ask

> I've gambled on many individuals whose enthusiasm, energy, and passion proved to be much more valuable to Jazzercise than their previous work experience may have indicated.
>
> —*Judi Sheppard Missett*

yourself, "What's fun or interesting about my business?" Then, run with it!

Finally, don't let money be your motivation. Instead, let it be a love for what you do and a desire to make a difference. My decisions are not driven by profit. I try to think of how much fun I'm going to have with a particular decision and whether it will create a win–win situation for everyone involved. In my experience, money follows ideas, not vice versa.

There you have it, my formula for business success. I'd like to leave you with this final thought: Winners are never surprised when they win. Positive thinking, energy, and enthusiasm are always contagious. And whatever you do, try to get one heck of a kick out of it!

JUDI'S 10 ACTION STEPS TO SUCCESS

1. Choose a career that ignites your passion.
2. See every roadblock as an opportunity.
3. Be willing to continue learning and changing to keep pace with our ever-evolving society.
4. Don't lose sight of your core purpose/mission.
5. Listen to your customers and employees—they are a wonderful resource for new ideas!
6. Surround yourself with good people and trust them to make decisions.
7. Strike a balance between your personal and business lives.
8. Conduct yourself and your business with honesty, fairness, and integrity.
9. Trust your instincts; gather the information you need, but don't ignore your gut feeling.
10. Think big and create excitement!

About the Author

As president and CEO of Jazzercise, **Judi Sheppard Missett** has created a dynamic fitness program that has grown to international prominence. In addition to providing business opportunities to thousands of Jazzercise franchisees, Judi has advanced the cause of preventive health care by promoting regular physical exercise. She has lent her leadership and expertise to industry associations, such as the National Fitness Leaders Association and the California Governor's Council on Physical Fitness and Sports. She has participated in a wide range of philanthropic and community service events, and has received numerous honors, including three Presidential commendations, the IDEA Lifetime Achievement Award, and *Working Woman* magazine's prestigious Harriet Alger Award, which honors the achievements, vision, and leadership of an entrepreneurial woman.

Judi Sheppard Missett
President and CEO
Jazzercise, Inc.
2460 Impala Drive
Carlsbad, CA 92008
Phone: (760) 476-1750, 1-800-FIT-IS-IT
Fax: (760) 602-7180
E-mail: *jazzinc@jazzercise.com*
Web site: *www.jazzercise.com*

chapter two

The Craft of Choosing Well: The Ultimate Key to Success

Eileen McDargh
President, McDargh Communications

Wealth is the product of a person's capacity to think.

—Ayn Rand

From our careers to our lifestyles, from our life partners to our life's legacy, we have a vast array of possibilities facing us. Our ability to think clearly and to make wise choices in our lives has everything to do with creating a world of our own choosing. To me, that is the ultimate success.

With a degree in communications, my career life began in education and quickly moved to marketing and advertising in the business world. An avocation in psychology and a stint in journalism allowed me to quickly pick up the nuances of an enterprise. I worked as the head of marketing for an internationally recognized real estate development and resort property. I handled corporate and investor relations for a health care corporation. I became a public relations consultant responsible for multinational companies. And I fried. I burned. I sizzled out in one big heap of misery and unhappiness. Something just wasn't right!

I left. I opened up my own company. I had learned the first skill in choosing well: Know what you don't want.

Practice Reverse Goal Setting

The admonition to "set goals" is all well and good. But for many of us setting goals is simply not "do-able." Why? Because we don't have a clear idea of what we want.

Through trial and error I have found real benefit in practicing what I call "reverse goal setting." Specifically, sit down with pen and paper and begin to itemize all the things you truly do not want in your life. Begin with your career. With mine, I knew that I did not want to write another press release. I knew that I did not want to take certain clients because I understood, in my heart of hearts, we truly could not serve them in the best fashion. I knew that I did not want someone else controlling what I delivered in exchange for money. I did not want to be hamstrung by corporate politics, or by the hours on a clock that translated "face time" as the only measure of value.

> Successful people not only have goals, they have goals that are meaningful for them.
>
> —*Marsha Sinetar*

Try writing reverse goals for the other areas of your life as well. Be sure to include the physical, emotional, material, and spiritual dimensions.

Once you begin to write reverse ("I don't want . . .") goals, spelling out clearly and authentically what you know you don't want, an amazing thing happens: you begin to realize what you do want. I realized that I wanted to be my own boss in a creative endeavor that makes a difference in the world. I realized that I wanted to exercise and to practice the nutrition essential for health. I wanted a life partner with a strong sense of self-esteem, humor, and a capacity to love deeply and widely. I wanted to give whatever I want as gifts and live in a place that nurtures me with its beauty and peace. And I wanted to be engaged in a spiritual quest.

Now let me share with you the other key to this process: You must chart your course for the journey.

Determine Your "True North" Based on Values

When I lecture on the concepts in my book, *Work for a Living and Still Be Free to Live*, I ask participants to close their eyes, hold one hand over their heads, and on the count of three, to point to where they think "true north" lies. When they open their eyes, they see fingers pointed in every direction. And everyone in that room is absolutely correct. Each of us has our own "true north."

I think of life as a journey, a sailing voyage to be exact. Decisions to help us stay on course must be based on both our individual sailboat as well as the chart we navigate. If we haven't charted a course, all the navigation skill in the world will still put us in the wrong place. So we need to chart our course, and there is a handy process for this. I look at it as a formula, whereby we can take stock of our decisions by weighing them against our personal values.

> The seafaring man who follows the waters follows the stars. And if you use them as your guides, you can reach your destiny.
>
> —*Carl Schurz*

> **Step 1:** Determine what is of value to you. Value has more to do with who you are and how you live your life than with what you have achieved. For example, you might value lifelong learning, financial security, service to others, loving relationships, and spiritual growth. Once you have identified

what is of value, you have a screen through which you can filter your goals and activities.

One of the best ways to identify values is to create an imaginary sounding board composed of four to five people whom you value and admire and who, in turn, sincerely respect and like you. If each one were to give your eulogy, what type of person would they say you were and why? What values arise? What goals or activities support those values? Isolate those values and write them down. You might even be able to rank-order the values.

Step 2: For a period of one week, keep a pad of paper handy and make a note of every task you perform and what role you play. For example, my roles are professional speaker, writer, wife, mother, friend, office worker, manager, daughter, sister, student, volunteer, and just plain me. The last refers to a role that nurtures and cares for me, not necessarily anyone else. Amazingly, I've discovered that every task is related to a role and that almost all tasks come in 15-minute increments.

Step 3: On a scale from minus 5 to plus 5, rate the roles you've identified in step 2 and their accompanying tasks according to enjoyment and personal value. In looking at your tasks of the week, you may make interesting discoveries. Are the various tasks and roles you've played congruent with the values you've identified? Are you putting more time than is reasonable into some tasks and roles? The operative word here is "reasonable." For example, I discovered that I was putting far too much time into the role of "office worker" at the expense of the role of "manager." Instead of assigning tasks and growing others, I was taking on work that did not need to be done by me. Time to alter course and allow my associates to hold the tiller.

Finally, by putting so much emphasis on the role of professional speaker and its tasks, I had let me drop. Time to make decisions for overhaul and repair, saying "yes" to a day off, to a day of contemplative silence. I realized that without allowing myself a time of silence, all I bring to the platform and my audiences are echoes of words rather than insights. Let me say that again, "without allowing myself a time of silence." This is another essential ingredient in the craft of choosing well: allowing time for silent retreat.

> Silence isn't golden. It's power.
>
> —*Tamala Edwards*

Retreat in Order to Advance

The more faithfully you listen to the voice within you, the better you will hear what is sounding outside. And only she who listens can speak.

—DAG HAMMARSKJÖLD

Many of us have difficulty with being alone. And silence scares us. In a world constantly bombarding us with sound, some of us promptly turn on the television or radio as soon as we enter an empty house. I have discovered the deep necessity for silence and alone time. Even if it means checking into a local motel, unplugging the phone, and ordering room service, choosing well demands that we spend time thinking and writing in the silence. Yes, writing.

When thoughts stay only in our heads, I am convinced we do not receive their full power. The writing is for you alone. Use a spiral notebook, a blank book, or a yellow pad. But write in ink.

Write the question you are trying to answer. Write, free-form, all your thoughts and fears and dreams about that question. Wake up in the middle of the night and record a dream you have. In the morning, read it back. Keep the notebook. Pick it up after some time has passed. You will be amazed at the wisdom found there—wisdom that sometimes we don't get on the first reading of our words. If you wish to learn more about journaling as a method for self-discovery, check out the Intensive Journal Workshops offered around the United States by facilitators trained in the Progoff Journal Workshop method.

> The art and science of asking questions is the source of all knowledge.
>
> —Dr. Adolf Berle

Experience the Call of the Wild

John O'Donohue in his book *Eternal Echoes* writes:

> When you find a place in Nature where the heart and mind find rest, then you have discovered a sanctuary for your soul. Nature calls us to tranquillity and rhythm. When your heart is confused or heavy, a day outside in Nature's quiet eternity restores your lost tranquillity.

In the creative process, there is a stage called incubation. Answers arise after a period of gestation, a period marked by not actively discussing the problem but rather letting the mind focus elsewhere. Nature is the perfect gestation place for seeking wisdom about our choices. In the call of the wild, it is possible to find clarity that's unavailable in the confusion and activity of our homes and offices.

For me, experiencing the call of the wild does not mean that you have to go backpacking in the High Sierra, though this is certainly an option. Rather, I am talking about taking mini-retreats in whatever natural setting is close by and calls to you. My best friend walks in the cemetery near her house. There, amid the trees and flowers and grasses, wending her way around the headstones placed more for the living than for the deceased, she finds peace and clarity.

I live near the ocean. I place a problem requiring a decision in the back of my mind and I walk. On more than one occasion, as the ocean's foam scuds at my tennis shoes, it has delivered up one of its treasures, replete with timely metaphorical meaning for me. Powerful messages from the wild.

Find whatever place calls to you and take the time to go there, with ears and eyes wide open. I am confident you will receive the information you need.

Know Your Season and Grow Your Season

There is the wonderful line in the Bible (Ecclesiastes 3:1) that says, "To everything there is a season and a time for every purpose under heaven." Our ability to choose well also rests on how truthful we are about the "season" of our life. If we are at the beginning of our career, our marriage, our family, choices will need to take these things into account. I remember how I thrilled to the excitement and challenge of my first job after leaving teaching. I loved the adult company, the ability to be creative, and the challenge of so many things to learn. I accepted requests to do anything and everything because I was learning. Today, I am more selective about the tasks I take on— asking now if they further the larger goals I have chosen.

> Saying no can be the ultimate self-care.
>
> —*Claudia Black*

Our bodies also have a season. I have discovered that, unlike many of my colleagues, for me nonstop travel is exhausting and not fun. My body requires seven hours of sleep, regular exercise, and downtime. I can take only so many back-to-back engagements before I must say "No." Trusting that I can say "No" is a lesson I have struggled to learn.

Accept Irresistible Offers

"Irresistible" means that without a doubt I want to say "Yes" and that the request comes without force or compromise from the source or me. There is no emotional blackmail, no "should," no social obligation. Irresistible requests are gifts to be gratefully accepted. If our time is filled only with "resistible" demands, how will we ever be able to accept the irresistible? I've determined that there are other critical questions that can help us determine if a choice is irresistible.

1. Does it support my values of lifelong learning and making a difference? Will it stop another person from growing? Will it stretch my abilities?
    I recently accepted an assignment that will cost time, money, and effort as well as time away from home. I accepted it because it will move me into trying something that I have never done before . . . an activity directly related to my role of professional speaking and service.
2. Does it allow me to be with people whom I care about?
    How often have we all said "Yes" to an engagement because we felt "guilty," when the reality is that we found the people tedious, demanding, or downright boring? I have finally determined that, as I have limited time to spend with my family and friends, it is perfectly fine to periodically decline such invitations.
3. Is it fun and will it allow for creativity and a change of pace?
4. Will it create organization and structure in my life? Am I the only one who can do this?
5. Is it authentic to me and of service to others?

I was asked if I would run for the board of directors of a nonprofit organization. Knowing I have strong organizational and leadership abilities, not to mention an ego, saying "Yes" to serve the organization's membership seemed appropriate. However, when I tested the request against the other questions just listed, more negative responses appeared. I turned down the nomination.

Think "Give," Not "Get"

Experience has taught me that when we make choices *to give* because it is the right thing to do, without any thought of getting back in return, we do receive in full measure.

Easy to do? No. When we are the bill payers, it is so easy to get tapped into the mentality of scarcity, wondering just how much different actions will cost us. So practice small. My beloved brother-in-law, Noam Pitlik, always said, "It's only money." His decisions to give time and resources to his colleagues, his family, and his "customers" gave him not only a fabulous career as an Emmy Award–winning director, but also earned him the love and devotion of a wide Hollywood community.

> There is no lasting happiness in having or getting, but only in giving.
>
> —*Henry Drummond*

Invest in the Future

The craft of choosing well demands that we take also a long-term view of our work and life. Investing in the future can mean everything from education to people to actual investments. It can mean choosing to spend time with our family and community because the future rests in their hands. As a grandmother, I have made a deliberate choice to spend at least one week every other month with my granddaughters who live in Oregon. Since I live in Southern California, this is no small effort, and yet the investment in our relationship and their future is well worth that effort.

Celebrate Daily and Give Thanks

> *No pessimist ever discovered the secrets of the stars or sailed to an uncharted land or opened a new heaven to the human spirit.*
>
> —HELEN KELLER

There is much to be thankful for. We simply cannot be pessimists if we are constantly focused on gratitude. Gratitude opens the heart and mind, making it possible for us to see more than what sits before our eyes. Gratitude also has the unique ability to soothe the edges of our disappointment and fear. When we realize the many riches that exist in our lives, we feel stronger, more confident, and in control. Sarah ban Breathnach was right when she recommended keeping a gratitude journal. Without fail, I daily write five things that occurred that day for which I am grateful. Even on the bleakest of days, this practice has carried me through.

In Conclusion

The craft of choosing well, a craft that only improves over time and with practice, is guaranteed to create ultimate success. Our ultimate success is to live our lives by design, not by default. When we practice the skill of choosing well, we come to see and to experience the opportunities and events of our lives in a different light than ever before. Only authentic decisions allow us to do what we truly love and to stay in love with what we do.

THE CRAFT OF CHOOSING WELL— 10 STEPS TO ULTIMATE SUCCESS

1. Practice reverse goal setting.
2. Determine your "true north" based on values.
3. Retreat in order to advance.
4. Experience the call of the wild.
5. Know your season and grow your season: control the controllable.
6. Accept irresistible offers.
7. Think "give," not "get."
8. Invest in the future.
9. Celebrate daily.
10. Give thanks.

About the Author

With more than 20 years of experience as a professional speaker, author, and management consultant, **Eileen McDargh** has worked with organizations and associations throughout the United States, Canada, and the Pacific Rim. Her ability to connect with mind, heart, and spirit makes her one of the most sought after keynoters, workshop leaders, and facilitators.

She draws upon practical business know-how, life experience, and years of consulting to national and international organizations to help audiences learn leadership, manage change, and achieve balance in their work and their lives. Her clients include global organizations in health care, education, the public sector, finance, and insurance, as well as a wide variety of associations. Author of *Work for a Living and Still Be Free to Live*, Eileen is a frequent contributor to numerous business journals and newsmagazines and has appeared several times on *CNN Headline News*.

Eileen McDargh
McDargh Communications
33465 Dosinia Drive
Dana Point, CA 92929
Phone: (949) 496-8640
Fax: (949) 248-7805
E-mail: *mcdargh@aol.com*
Web site: *www.eileenmcdargh.com*

chapter three

Position Yourself for Incredible Success

JANET LAPP, R.N., PH.D.
President, CLD International

If your model for "normal" is the 1960s, '70s, or '80s, you will never get back to normal. "Normal" is based on a whole set of global economic conditions that no longer apply.

The traditional career path has dead-ended. In 2001, only one person in every 50 will be promoted, compared to one in 20 in 1987. By 2002, 85 percent of the United States labor force will be working for firms employing fewer than 200 people. Only 39 percent of employed persons state that they intend to be in the same job in five years.

The contract between employer and employee may have changed forever. Ray Smith, CEO of Bell Atlantic, has said, "Once in the corporation,

1. Start preparing yourself and your department as if it, and you, were already outsourced.
2. Begin to think like an entrepreneur. Track your income and expenses. Ask daily how you can increase revenue and cut costs.
3. Plan and execute your sales and marketing campaign to let others in the company know about your services.

the employee's own skills, talent, and personality must bring them to the fore, because the corporation isn't really tracking people." Bell Atlantic's training courses are now stored in their computers, and employees are responsible for learning what's available and mastering the content. Job openings are listed in the computer, and employees are responsible for knowing what's available and applying for the position. Most importantly, at Bell Atlantic employees are responsible for increasing their value to the company. There's nothing in Smith's message about taking care of employees. Being taken care of will not be part of the new corporate commitment. This means that an increase in employee self-interest is necessary at the same time that organizations need a commitment to optimizing the good of the whole.

How to Keep Your Job

Perception is all there is. Take charge of building the right perceptions. You start as an expense item at the beginning of the day. By the end of the day, what have you added as value? You must add value and be able to communicate that value so that it is clearly perceived and will be remembered.

1. Promote Yourself. Make Yourself Indispensable.

You are in charge of building perceptions about yourself. People know little about you, and much of that information may be inaccurate. Constantly inform people about yourself and your product or service.

2. PUSH YOUR IDEAS THROUGH AND GET CREDIT FOR THEM.

Many people hate to self-promote because it's "self-centered," it is not in keeping with their professional image, or they feel they shouldn't have to. They think, "If I'm excellent and work hard, they'll notice and reward me." The truth is that many of us work hard, put in long hours, and then wake up in midcareer and realize: there's no snooze alarm on our biological clocks; the Marlboro man died of cancer; Snow White was a snow job; we're not as effective as we'd like; and our positions are in jeopardy.

- Find allies within your company who will support your ideas.
- If you're blocked just ahead, go through someone else.
- Think through your idea thoroughly before presenting it. Why is the idea good? How does it fit in with corporate strategy? Is it worth the risk and cost?
- What resources and skills does the company need?
- Never ask for a decision larger than the one you need.
- Undercommit and overperform.

Look for the troublemakers.

—PETER DRUCKER

All progress is the result of unreasonable men and women.

—GEORGE BERNARD SHAW

3. BE MATURE.

Even if you have skills and position yourself well in the company, you can still derail. Moving through corporate ladders and chains requires more than ever before. You might need to demonstrate time and again how well you can get along with other people. If you have not done so already, plan to develop the interpersonal skills that are clear marks of maturity:

a. Accept responsibility. Only the pope is infallible . . . and then only occasionally. If you've made a mistake, admit it; you'll be admired, not rebuked. Don't try to shift blame to someone else. Such behavior is a sign of immaturity.

b. Let others be right. Coworkers won't tolerate you for long if you have a high need to be right, or if you tell them, "I told you so," or "Why didn't you take my advice?" State your opinion as opinion, not as fact.

c. Trust. Business runs on trust. Prying into other people's business and casting doubt on their motives and intentions destroys trust. Give others the benefit of the doubt. Create trust by doing what you say you'll do.

d. Give first. Show a willingness to help others before you expect others to help you.

e. Support others' accomplishments. Send compliments up as well as down. When someone does an outstanding job, make sure the employee knows it—and make sure your boss knows it as well. Note small things that people do right, and congratulate them at the moment they do them.

Important Trends to Track

In addition to being selective about what work you do and developing personal success skills, consider these trends as you position yourself:

1. Small and medium-size companies are the engines of job creation. Small companies will be handling the work outsourced by the giants. New technology lets the nimbler and more innovative of the companies compete against the giants better than ever before. Become familiar with smaller

companies within your area of expertise. Your future may be brighter there.

2. The big corporation of the future will consist of a small core of central employees, with a mass of smaller firms working for it under contract. Even within the central core, there will be continuous shifting around and hiring of people for specific, temporary assignments. If you are flexible and have good skills, you may be better off in this new environment than you are now.

   If your department is outsourced and you are offered another position in the company or even laid off, you have the option of starting your own company. Jump-start your business by contracting with your former employer as your first customer.

3. Be prepared to work for a foreign company and in a foreign land. Or start that foreign company yourself. Corporations are contracting to have operations carried out at lower cost overseas. For example, New York Life has some claims processing handled by employees in Ireland. You may increase your chances of working abroad by learning a foreign language. If you work at this language diligently, daily, for only 15 minutes per day, you can become functionally fluent within a year.

4. Gear yourself toward starting your own company or working for another woman. Women entrepreneurs are starting companies at one-and-a-half times the rate of men. In 1972, 3 percent of the work force was employed by women. Currently, that figure is 12 percent, with the near-future forecast at 25 percent. There are now more new jobs being created by women than by all the *Fortune* 500 companies.

5. Get as much education as possible. The future belongs to the knowledgeable worker. People who get paid well in the future will have clearly definable skills, and knowledge that immediately translates to profit.

6. Keep upgrading your skills. Expect to change careers—not just jobs—three or four times during your working life. Keep your resume current. Skills required by the new technologically driven organizations can be learned at

community colleges, in apprenticeship programs, or with on-the-job training. Many programs are government supported as well.

What you earn depends on what you learn.

Many of today's career options were either not available to, or not acceptable by, women only a few short years ago. Today, knowledge in these career areas will give any woman a razor-sharp advantage.

Option 1: Finance. Finance is the core of so many companies that no woman can afford to avoid schooling in it. Master the math you hated in high school. This will help you understand, among other things, how your company raises and allocates capital. It will also make clear why that new product your team has designed might not be launched. Some of the most talented and valued corporate officers are the new breed of financial officer, and there are too few women in this position.

Option 2: Accounting. Managers who know how to read a balance sheet or a profit-and-loss statement are at an advantage. If you're not among that group, sign up for a course in these fundamentals.

Option 3: Computers. Knowing the basics of word processing and spreadsheets is essential. The ability to navigate the Internet is fast becoming essential as well. If the best you can do is run the spell checker on your word processor, it's time to update. Be able to set up home pages on the World Wide Web and create interactivity among and between them.

Option 4: Sales and Marketing. Learn how to target a market, capitalize on brand equity, position a product, and use market research techniques.

Option 5: Communication. Technical expertise will get you further if you can express yourself to customers, colleagues, journalists, and the public.

Skills and Values Audit

According to William Bridges in *Job Shift* (Addison-Wesley, 1994), we will have several different sources of income from several different skill sets in the employment scenario of the near future. Instead of identifying with your job or your profession, spend the time to identify your skills and values.

It is extremely important that your identification of self be very solid around values (what is important to you, your mission or meaning), and skills (all that you are able to do), and less around profession or job. For example, a registered nurse is a highly skilled professional who, because of health-care reform, has been forced to rethink his or her professional definition. The old thinking is "I am a registered nurse in the Critical Care Unit." The new thinking is "I value helping others and creating health. My skills are observation, rapid deductive and inductive reasoning, scanning, intuition, quick mental reflexes, an understanding of networks and systems, natural instincts for teaching as well as healing, and the ability to learn, maintain, enhance, and use highly technical knowledge." If this nurse needs to give up the title of nurse and a job in patient care, what do her values and skills allow her to do? Become a case manager? Health-care network facilitator? Consultant? They are all equally valid as ways of using her already developed gifts, values, and skills as they have been described.

1. Create initiatives in which you can demonstrate your value.
2. Make sure you have breadth, and at least one area of depth.
3. Position yourself so you're a key player in the loop.
4. Become a person whose views are respected.
5. Be selective: accept only the assignments that give you the best opportunity to work from your strengths.
6. Do work that lets you say, "In 2001, I was responsible for gaining x number of customers, saving y number of dollars, increasing revenues by z."

What Are Your Skills and Values?

There are several initial steps to identifying your skills and values. The following are some of the simplest and most straightforward:

- Think of what you enjoy doing the most. Make a list of the top three.
- Think about what you loved to do as a kid. Write or draw it out.
- What do you stand for? Name one thing you are willing to die for.
- Ask yourself: Who really wants me to work at the job I have now? What did people early in my life advise me to do? What was important to my parents? Was it education? Appearances? Wealth? Are my occupations and relationships reflecting this? Is this what I want?
- When you procrastinate, what do you do? Often, this is what you have talent or deep interest in doing, and can more easily develop into a passion. Write down a couple of suggestions for turning this procrastination into a career or useful pastime.
- Ask your friends or colleagues what they think your natural talent is.
- Imagine your life on video as it will appear five years from now, after you have settled into your new lifestyle and your risk is realized. These exercises will help draw you toward self-actualization.

Complete these sentences. Each of them will help you focus on your true desires and natural talents:

- Someday I would really love to . . .
- If I could, I would . . .
- I have always wanted to . . .
- Wouldn't it be wonderful if I . . .

Do not complain that you cannot see the sunset.
Build your house with windows facing west.

—Old Proverb

If You Have Reorganized

If you have experienced a recent reorganization, or several of them, here are some suggestions for how to refocus your energies to adapt to the new system.

1. Find out your company's new priorities, and realign your job responsibilities to them. Stop doing work that doesn't pay off for you or the company, such as busywork, unneeded steps, and duties that contribute nothing.
2. Take on new responsibilities that are also high payoff for you. If you are becoming burned out, try to keep committed anyway. If you can't give 100 percent effort, cut back on how much you do, not on the percentage effort with which you do it.
3. If you think you'll find a company that works you less than yours, happy hunting. There are constant changes in every company, not just yours.
4. Don't wait for someone else to make things clearer or easier, or to lighten your pressure. Pressure is increasing, not decreasing. Take steps to organize yourself. Create clarity in your own work area. You know your company's vision, so create the steps you need to take to help it realize that vision.
5. It's not that your company doesn't care; they are doing what they're doing to survive. If you blame someone else, or feel like a victim, move off it. It doesn't help your job situation, or your well-being, to be negative.
6. Your company has to change fast. The more people head in the same direction, the faster the change. When your company makes a decision, practice switching fast instead of digging in your heels.

Prepare for Job Loss

Don't play it safe. Always be ready to leave.

Regardless of how much power you think you have, the corporate climate has changed so much that it's reasonable to expect that you can lose your position overnight. Here are some exercises that could well make the prospect of job loss less painful:

1. Get paid at least once for a skill or hobby outside your current job. Identify the skills you could turn to over the next six months if you needed to. Attempt to win at least one client for your services. Psychologically, it is important that you are paid: when you have done it once, you believe you can do it again.

    The package we create provides the income that we make.

2. Live well below your income for a month. Excluding housing, budget and live at 25 percent of your current income. Typically, the large expenses that need to be cut are the ones that you took on to prove to others that you could afford them, not the ones that give you joy. Many people find after this exercise that they begin to want to give up status objects and appearances.

3. Liquidate on paper everything you have: house, car, equipment, investments. Call a real estate agent in a town or city with a major university and less expensive living costs. You'll find that to rent a good town house costs very little. Apply 40 percent of your liquidated assets to your living costs. You can live an acceptable lifestyle in a good community for many years with the other 60 percent. Being trapped by money is psychological. We are programmed to achieve in order to please others, so we're convinced that external symbols of success are what draw people to us.

Those who can see the bridges can cross them more easily. People who visualize alternatives handle transitions more easily.

4.　Ask your partner and children to list the things that they like and don't like about you, and how you could improve your relationship with them. They won't mention your job or your money, but rather your companionship, your love, and your happiness. Keep their lists and read them whenever you need to comfort and remind yourself that if you lost everything they will love you anyway.

5.　Write your own obituary. Make it long and glowing—what you would like your mother, father, or favorite teacher to read about you. Think about when you are gone and what you would like to hear about yourself in your obituary, as compared to what it would say today given the life plan you are currently following.

As Lily Tomlin put it: "The trouble with the rat race is, even if you win it, you are still a rat." Your life is not your career. Change your perspective. Your career should be about living your life your way, or as Dewitt Jones, *National Geographic* photographer, has said, "Make your life your art." The world cannot take away anything unless you give it the power to do so by making the external world your source.

If You and Your Job Are Separated

Consider whether or not you could be a consultant if you found yourself between paid positions. Even if this scene is inapplicable to you, preparing yourself to become a consultant is a valuable exercise to sharpen skills and focus talents.

You may do well as a consultant if you:

- Have a deep understanding of a product, service, job, or industry—even better if this knowledge/experience is in demand or is unique

- Have been exposed to many different work environments, or one or two in detail
- Have participated in, or observed, the formation and implementation of business decisions
- Are self-motivated and can work without an external stimulus

When you are sure of the change or of leaving your job, here are steps to consider:

1. Rather than focus on job experience, take stock of your values and skills. Develop them and list examples of them.
2. Join a professional association. Associations are our modern guilds. Not only will you be able to connect with others for future referrals, your association is up-to-date on developments in your area of experience and can guide you to more resources within your company or town.
3. Computerize yourself. This computer trend is not going to pass. Current technology skill is essential to be perceived as a good hire. In fact, one of the fastest growing areas of opportunity is in helping customers to become techno-literate and to establish an Internet presence.
4. Put out the word that you are going out on your own. Personal contacts within your industry are a proven source of customers, as are published articles in trade journals and periodicals. My experience is that most editors are grateful for new material and will welcome your article. Once you are published, you are, rightly or wrongly, considered "an expert."
5. Give speeches to conventions, trade associations, and service clubs. Join Toastmasters and finish at least the first level of competency. Call local Rotary, Kiwanis, and Lions clubs to offer a program on a useful business topic.
6. Send out press releases to trade and local papers. One interview can earn lots of mileage. There is a book of media contacts for most towns, and a book of national media contacts in your local library.

7. Keep moving, challenging yourself, and planting seeds. Success takes time.

Summary

You are responsible for your own career, regardless of the actions of the company for whom you work. There are numerous options available to you, and many of them reside just outside the boundaries of your current thinking. Your smartest move is to reorient your focus away from your "job" and toward your skills. And happy hunting—this is a fantastic time for women!

10 Action Steps to Success

1. Position yourself so you're a key player in the loop.
2. Prepare for job loss now.
3. Be selective in accepting assignments that give you an opportunity to shine.
4. Do work that lets you say, "In 1996, I was responsible for gaining x number of customers, saving y number of dollars, increasing revenues by z."
5. Promote yourself. Make yourself indispensable.
6. Start preparing yourself as if you were already outsourced.
7. Begin to think like an entrepreneur.
8. Get as much education as possible. Upgrade your skills.
9. Learn another language.
10. Do a *Skills and Values* audit.

About the Author

Janet Lapp, Ph.D., is the author of *Plant Your Feet Firmly in Mid-Air* and *Dancing with Tigers,* and was creator and host of the highly rated CBS series *Keep Well.* A Canadian now based in San Diego, California, Janet was a registered nurse and nurse manager before completing a Ph.D. with Honours from McGill University in Montreal. Awarded a postdoctoral fellowship, she went on to a successful career as a clinician and university professor. Now an award-winning speaker, she is president of CLD International and the publisher of *The Change Letter,* a trend-tracking guide to common-sense change. Dr. Janet Lapp is now one of North America's most celebrated speakers. Her exhilarating programs provide real and effective strategies that can be put to work right away in helping people adapt to the fast changing world of work.

Dr. Janet Lapp, President
CLD International
P.O. Box 1882
Rancho Santa Fe, CA 92067
Phone: (858) 759-7334
Fax: (858) 759-7346
E-mail: *DrJanet@Lapp.com*
Web site: *www.lapp.com*

chapter four

Quest for Your Best: The Four Stages to Achieving Success

LORNA RILEY
President, American Training Association

In Search of Success

What is it that you want? Where is it that you want to go? What will make you happy? How do you become successful?

These are some of the questions we wrestle with throughout a lifetime. A fortunate few know what they want and how to get it. Those charmed people set a course and achieve extraordinary results under the same circumstances in which others are left in the dust. Why? *Because they know the way.* Do any of these refrains sound familiar?

1. "I'd be really good at *something*, if I just knew what it was."
2. "Things haven't worked out like I thought they would."
3. "Life has passed me by."
4. "I want to know that the struggle means *something*."

These are some of the frustrations people all around us experience every day. They occur when there's a gap between where we are and where we'd like to be. Most of the time we're quiet about this gap—resigned to living a life which Thoreau called one "of quiet desperation." But sometimes it wells up and breaks open on us in the form of broken relationships, job-hopping, neurosis, or even worse.

Although these times are difficult, they also serve as useful red flags because they point out to us what we do not want in our lives. They identify our pain, which in turn can become the spark for setting new goals for ourselves. If you're frustrated over a job, for example, that frustration is an important clue about a job that you probably don't want. If you decide to do something about it, you're making a move toward your success—getting what you *do* want. The problem is solved when you close the gap between where you are and where you want to be. Sounds simple—and it is. It's simple, but not easy.

> *What is success? I think it is a mixture of having a flair for the thing that you are doing; knowing that it is not enough, that you have got to have hard work and a certain sense of purpose.*
>
> —MARGARET THATCHER

What You Need in Order to Be Successful

What we need in order to be successful is *a way to get there!* We need a game plan . . . a strategy . . . or what I call a "road map." Success does not happen by chance. The best intentions will not get us there. Pure motivation and passion will not get us there. Eventually we need to take our passion out onto the road for a test drive.

When I became a professional speaker and trainer, my work allowed me to study many skills for professional and personal development. I wrote and delivered dozens of diverse programs. Over time, however, I felt as if I were repeating myself. I was teaching different subjects, *but the process for reaching the result was always the same!* Not only that, I also discovered that this process was simply the oldest story known to humankind. It was nothing more or less than "the heroic journey," the single thread common to all cultures and mythologies since the dawn of humanity, according to the eminent scholar Joseph Campbell.

> When you're going through hell, keep on going.
>
> —*Lorna Riley*

The heroic journey goes like this: We all have a starting place or comfort zone. According to mythic archetypes, we leave it willing or unwillingly. If we leave it willingly, it's to achieve a goal or fulfill a mission. Then we find helpers to guide us. We make action plans and then put them to the test. We face challenges, and if we've done the right stuff, we achieve the goal or payoff.

I call these four stages Home, Help, Challenge, and Prize. You could just as well call them Village (Home), Mentor (Help), Dragon Slaying (Challenge), and Damsel Saving (Prize). But we're not done yet. To complete the cycle, we must return Home—back to the village to share our bounty and begin again. The hero's journey then, is a time-tested strategy, a road map, to get us where we want to go.

If you follow the road map's four-stage process, not only will you solve the problem and achieve your goal, but you will experience *nine* other benefits as well. You will also become a successful risk taker, personal leader, change manager, project manager, self-learner, and scientific inquisitor, as well as perhaps more spiritually evolved and able to accomplish all this while in a state of flow. Now, that's what I call a success! You went looking for one thing, and

> Fortune's expensive
> smile is earned.
>
> —*Emily Dickinson*

wound up with nine other rewards as well! Let's take a look at the four stages that get us where we want to go.

The Four Stages Required for Success
Stage 1: Home

There are homes you run from and homes you run to.

—LAURA CUNNINGHAM

Home is our comfort zone and the starting place for your journey. It is a metaphor in the road map for those comfort zones we settle into, whether they're in our living arrangements, careers, relationships, politics, or thinking. Home is our place of security, safety, and comfort.

The irony of Home is that while it's comforting, it can also numb us into complacency. We lose interest, get lazy, or accept our situations without challenge or question. Sometimes the allure of keeping the status quo is so strong that no matter how difficult or painful the situation, we choose to do nothing. Home can be a painful place, numbed by routine.

By definition, however, life is a dynamic, changing force. If we want to truly reap the rewards life has to offer, we must accept the call to adventure and keep our lives vital by learning and growing. To do that, we will need to leave Home. Here are five ways to leave:

1. ASK QUESTIONS

Questions begin the "quest," or search for answers. They disturb our thinking and shake our peace of mind. It may take some time, maybe years, to actually leave in search of the answers, but asking is a signal that begins the process. The more effective the questions, the more powerful the answers.

Always the more beautiful answer who asks a more beautiful question.

—E. E. CUMMINGS

I was once laid off twice in the same year. It was clear that what I was searching for—security—no longer existed in corporate America. I vowed that I would never again be dependent on anyone else for my security. I would have to find it by making my own way in the world.

My journey began by asking a powerful question. Instead of asking, "What do I want?" I asked, "What would be the *hardest* thing for me to do?" The answer was easy: public speaking. I had always been a shy, introspective person with a lot of enthusiasm. People misread that energy as outgoing, even though I was mush inside. Looking back, I was afraid of everything—afraid of losing, failing, risking, and rejection. I was even afraid of fear! I had never really put myself to the test. The final result of too much comfort and security is anxiety and paranoia about losing it.

> People seldom see the halting and painful steps by which the most insignificant success is achieved.
>
> —*Anne Sullivan*

2. IDENTIFY YOUR PAIN

Sometimes the "call to the quest" comes not through questions, but through pain. We go along and go along, dedicating ourselves to the satisfaction of pleasures, feeding the senses, gathering belongings, and seeking personal ambitions. We do the things we are "supposed to do." We marry, find work, have kids, go on vacations, read books, watch movies, find hobbies, and respond to life's vicissitudes. Then something happens, like a toothache in the middle of the night, and we hurt.

To identify what you want, look to your problems for clues. Problems cause pain. Wants are perceptions of something lacking. Identify your "lacking," or pain, and then imagine your ideal—your perfect life. Begin with "I am lacking _____" and fill in the blank. What you've just identified are seed goals. These form the embryos of your real goals. They identify opportunities to close the gap between where you are and where you want to be. Real goals are dreams with deadlines.

3. CREATE A VISION

It's been said that if we can see it, we can achieve it. Visions are pictures in our minds formed by our imaginations.

Visions contain two important properties: First, they reflect our *value and belief systems* of what's important to us. Like pain, they give us clues about what we seek. Second, they tend to be *future oriented*. They are pictures in our mind of the way things *could be*. When we mentally project ourselves into the future, we create imagined extensions of what our lives might look like. So imagine your ideal life, see the picture of it in your mind, and keep focused on it as you move through your journey.

4. LISTEN TO YOUR INNER "VOICE"

The "call" may also come in a very undramatic way, so untheatrical and quiet in fact that most of the time we miss its first attempts to get our attention. It is a small, faint inner voice whispering to our conscious mind.

Inner voices are the kinds of thoughts that can wake you out of a deep sleep, steer you clear of an accident, guide a decision, form a hunch, or get you excited about an idea. They will always tell you the truth.

If you hear the call, but remain stuck in a rut, check to see if any of these roadblocks apply to your situation:

- Fears
- Apathy
- Blame
- Self-limiting beliefs
- Laziness
- Negative self-talk
- Force of habit
- No mission
- No vision
- No curiosity
- Procrastination
- Refusal
- Lack of discipline
- Insufficient motivation
- Confusion
- Stubbornness
- Ignorance
- Indecision
- Need to follow the rules
- Perfectionism
- Mixed feelings
- Poor self-esteem
- Criticism
- Anxiety
- No support
- Lack of resources
- Hesitancy
- Poor health
- No money
- No time

Anything that can inhibit, will inhibit. How many of these could you control? Most of them.

> *If you think you can't, you won't. If you think you can, you will.*
>
> —LORNA RILEY

5. CREATE A MISSION

Now that you have asked questions, identified seed goals through your pain, created a vision of your ideal life, and listened to your inner voice, it's time to create a mission.

Write a short mission statement about what it is that you are seeking. Make it one sentence, easily understood, and able to be recited at gunpoint. Bill Gates: A laptop in every home. Joan of Arc: Save France. Mother Teresa: Comfort the sick. My mission statement for a second company I'm helping to establish: "Every learner online."

Stage 2: Help

> *You cannot shake hands with a clenched fist.*
>
> —GOLDA MEIR

Help is the stage where you look for helpers. Seldom is anything accomplished in isolation. Helpers can be people such as mentors, coaches, counselors, teachers, and role models. Helpers can also be things such as training, education, books, tapes, videos, tools, written goals, and the steps you list to get where you want to go. There are four steps for getting help.

> Good questions outperform easy answers every time.
>
> —*Lorna Riley*

STEP 1: IDENTIFY AND ENLIST HELPING PEOPLE

If you plan on reaching your goal sooner rather than later, find yourself someone who can guide you. It may be an official relationship with a coach, counselor, or mentor, or an unofficial helper whom you observe from afar. Good mentors and coaches can decrease your learning curve. They help you to see what needs to be done, and guide you along the way. The two (or more) of you working together will produce synergy. $1 + 1 = 5$!

STEP 2: IDENTIFY AND ENLIST HELPING RESOURCES

What tools do you need to achieve your goal? Do you need to go back to school? Learn from a book? Watch a video? Get a jigsaw?

When I first started in business, I served an apprenticeship working with a boss who taught me the tricks of the trade. I took notes on every tip he gave me and immediately implemented his ideas. Repeating his steps allowed me to become the instant top producer in his organization. Sometimes I would experiment and "turn off" the ideas. My sales immediately dropped. Without his guidance, I would have struggled in sales, and perhaps been too discouraged to begin my own professional speaking and training business.

STEP 3: SET GOALS

Go back to your list of seed goals and prioritize your list by what you feel is most urgent and important. Remember, the greater the pain, the more urgency it will have. Call that your "A" priority list. Go to work on those items first.

To turn your urgent and important seed goals into real goals, make them SMART. Write down a sentence that includes the following: S=specific (what do you want to accomplish?), M=measurable (how will you measure your achievement—if possible?), A=action-oriented (give your sentence a verb), R=be realistic about what you can do, and T=time-sensitive. The most important element of your goal sentence is to say *what* you hope to achieve, and by *when*. Example: I will start my own business by November 1.

> Make your life a mission, not an intermission.
>
> —*Arnold Glasgow*

STEP 4: LIST STEPS TO ACHIEVE YOUR GOAL(S)

Now make a list of all the baby steps you need to take in order to achieve your goal. Leave nothing out. Download your brain as fast as you can on paper, or talk into a tape recorder. Do not edit or try to organize your thoughts yet. Once you have everything identified, go back and organize them into a time sequence and assign a deadline for each. This becomes your step-by-step action planner, which is now ready for the next stage of the journey, called the Challenge.

Stage 3: The Challenge

Life is either a daring adventure or nothing.

—Helen Keller

Here's where you put your action plan to the test. In some ways this should be the easiest step because you've already done the hard part—you've left your comfort zone. Once you've left Home, sheer momentum will give you the courage to face this stage. If and when you're going through hell, keep going.

When I decided to open my own business, I felt confident that I could do it on my own because I had stopped and gotten Help from a mentor. My first action item for my goal was to get a business license. When reduced to a simple action, my focus was no longer on starting my own business. It was now a matter of getting in the car, driving to the city municipal building, and filling out some forms. I wrote out a check for $20 and, suddenly, I was in business. It wasn't frightening. It was exhilarating!

> Great opportunities to help others seldom come, but small ones surround us every day.
>
> *—Sally Koch*

Stage 4: The Prize

Luck is not chance, it's toil. Fortune's expensive smile is earned.

—Emily Dickinson

Some say they want money, prestige, glory, or fame in order to feel successful, but the biggest prizes are the ones you can't see or touch. They are intangibles such as healthy self-esteem, a sense of contribution, satisfaction of doing worthwhile work, and learning experiences.

The prize represents the point at which your problem is solved, even if that solution is only one baby step toward the ultimate solution. However small the risk, it is imperative to recognize that you have successfully taken it and become a personal leader of your own life. You have created a change, managed a project, learned lessons, and perhaps even enjoyed a spiritual evolution while you participated in your journey.

> Each moment is the great challenge, the best thing that ever happened to you.
>
> **—Grace Speare**

If you do not achieve the goal you identified at Home and Help, you still must collect a Prize. Don't go Home without one! Feedback, evaluation, reflection, and learning experiences are all forms of prizes. Look for what you didn't expect, and the gifts will be abundant.

> *Of all sad words of tongue or pen, the saddest are these: "it might have been!"*
>
> —JOHN GREENLEAF WHITTIER

Back Home to Journey Again

The journey does not stop at the Prize. You go home again and share your gifts. Teach others what you have learned, share your bounty with others. In so doing, you will discover a life of abundance instead of scarcity. You will reap successes beyond your wildest dreams, and finally find true balance. Balance is created by the centrifugal force of your continual participation in the journey's cycle. This whole process is about getting unstuck, and fully participating in the journey of life. It's good to have an end to the journey, but it's the journey that matters in the end. Here's what you may find along the way:

> Worthy prizes do not fall in your lap. You have to earn them.
>
> **—Lorna Riley**

- You searched for adventure to know the world.
- You found courage to know yourself.
- You searched for power to lead people.
- You found humility to understand greatness.
- You searched for wealth to be free from want.
- You found resourcefulness, which made you strong.
- You searched for energy to do great things.
- You found health in the peace of well-being.
- You searched for knowledge to spread the word.
- You found wisdom to illuminate the meaning.
- You searched for answers to understand why.
- You found questions that unlocked the truth.
- None that you had looked for . . . yet all that you had hoped for.
- You wanted success, and found life's treasures.

ROAD MAP TO CONTINUAL SUCCESS

Stage 1: Leave Home. Ask questions, identify your pain, create a vision, listen to your inner voice, and write a mission statement.

Stage 2: Get Help. Identify and enlist helping people and resources, set goals, and list steps with deadlines to achieve your goal(s).

Stage 3: Face the Challenge. Put your action plan to the test.

Stage 4: Collect Your Prize(s). Collect your learning experiences, gains, rewards, and feedback. Go Home and share them with others. Begin again. Enjoy the journey!

About the Author

Lorna Riley is founder and president of the American Training Association. A member of the National Speakers Association and the American Society of Training and Development, she brings a diverse background and high level of achievement to the podium with numerous awards to show for her success as a business owner, sales executive, and sales trainer. She has written several books: *Quest for Your Best: A Roadmap for Finding Fulfillment in a Challenging World, 76 Ways to Build a Straight Referral Business ASAP!, The Movie Lover's Cookbook: Reel Meals, Acts of Love, and Axe of Love*. She has also written and produced several cassette albums, including *The Power Pak: The Three Most Powerful Skills for Creating Success, Proactive Time Management*, and *Memory Management*. Lorna frequently contributes to trade publications and shares her unique philosophy of success in internationally known seminars, workshops, keynote presentations, and interviews with radio and TV audiences.

Lorna Riley, President
American Training Association
2455 Flametree Lane
Vista, CA 92084
Phone: (760) 639-4020
Fax: (760) 639-4023
E-mail: *Lorna@Lornariley.com*
Web site: *www.Lornariley.com*

chapter five

Presenting Your Best for Incredible Success: Skills for Presentation and Communication Excellence

MARY-ELLEN DRUMMOND
President, Polished Presentations International

*We are the painters of our own self-portraits. Who you become,
next week, next year, or five years from now, will be determined
by your attitude, your actions, and what you learn.*

—MARY-ELLEN DRUMMOND

My most embarrassing moments ever were watching a five-minute videotape of myself in a sales leadership assessment session. Seeing myself make
mistake after mistake was painful, but it was also a powerful lesson and a
turning point in my career and my life. Instantly I saw what I didn't like and

51

what I didn't want to be as a communicator. On the spot, I decided I had a new mission and I knew I had to change. It would be a huge mistake not to. I was motivated.

> Mistakes are part of the dues one pays for a full life.
>
> —*Sophia Loren*

And change I did. I eventually transformed my fear into excitement and learned to enjoy making presentations by studying the skills involved, preparing, and practicing. All those efforts paid off. Three years after my humbling video debut, I was named "Sales Representative of the Year" by the U.S. Pharmaceutical Division of Bristol Myers. Almost a decade later, I was inspired to start my own company, and I began my career as a full-time professional speaker. I know that I owe my success to learning from my mistakes and overcoming my fear of public speaking.

What do you think is the number one skill for achieving success? The ability to communicate effectively. And, what is Americans' number one fear? Public speaking, of course. Because public speaking is so feared, it is also a highly revered skill. When you improve your communication and presentation skills, your self-confidence and self-esteem will rise faster than if you develop any other skill. That's why it is to your advantage to polish your presentations. It will help you build your personal and professional success like nothing else.

> When you create a clear picture of the communicator you want to be, that's what you will eventually become.
>
> —*Mary-Ellen Drummond*

We're living in a very competitive, constantly changing, and challenging world where people are making faster and faster decisions about one another. Within seconds of meeting someone, we decide whether or not we like the person, whether or not we want to work with that person, and whether or not we trust that person. Our decisions are based on a quick evaluation of his or her confidence, competence, voice, body language, smile, sense of humor, eye contact, energy, attitude, and more.

This chapter gives you the self-presentation and communication techniques that will help you paint a self-portrait of the person you'd like to become by transforming your fear into excitement by strengthening your self-presentation and communication skills.

1. Know Who You Want to Be

There's an old saying that in every person there are two people: the person you are and the person you are capable of becoming. Until you evaluate yourself, or you ask a professional coach to do so, you won't know specifically what traits you could enhance, what skills you could develop, or what kind of communicator you could really become.

The most effective evaluation is going to be the most thorough. It probably isn't your idea of fun to be videotaped or audiotaped. But the tapes will capture the truth. Until you know what you do well and what you need to improve, you won't be able to get to where you want to go. By identifying your strengths and liabilities, you can begin to eliminate what you don't like and build on your best qualities, many of which you may not even be aware yet.

> Like deep sorrow or great love, nerves produce adrenaline which is what you have to use. I'd be frightened if I wasn't frightened.
>
> —*Academy Award–winning actress Judi Dench*

2. Say "Yes" and Transform Your Fear into Excitement

It's important to realize that it is absolutely normal to feel anxious when attention is focused on you, especially when you're called on to speak in front of others. To turn fear into excitement, ban the words "fear" and "nervous" from your vocabulary and replace them with "excitement," "excited," and "exciting." ("I'm excited about my program!") Your brain and body will believe what you say, so say something positive. Use your excitement and adrenaline rush to your advantage. Let's look at a few of the techniques that professional speakers use.

> You can only bring to life what you can imagine.

Just before you speak, remember to take at least two deep breaths. As you approach the front of the room, greet your introducer with a smile on your face. You'll feel more relaxed, and so will your audience.

Before you speak, pinch your fingers together (index finger, middle finger, and thumb) and hold that position tightly. As you release your pinched fingers after 30 seconds, your hands and arms will relax and you'll look far more confident.

If you experience "dry mouth," lightly bite your tongue. You will salivate and your cotton mouth will disappear.

3. Evaluate Your Current Skills and Style

In my seminars, I often play a 10-second audiocassette voice sample and then ask the audience to give me a rapid assessment of the anonymous person's taped voice. Reactions come instantly every time.

It is important to realize just how quickly people form negative or positive opinions about others. It is equally important to recognize that we do the same thing when assessing ourselves. We are our own worst critics, and we tend to decide quickly and irrevocably whether or not we're good at something.

> The trouble with most of us is that we would rather be ruined by praise than saved by criticism.
>
> —Dr. Norman Vincent Peale

But are we appraising ourselves accurately? I would offer that there's absolutely nothing to be gained by our lack of objectivity. So let's agree to take another look at ourselves—but with objectivity this time.

As a business professional you can learn from every meeting, training session, or conference by asking your audience members to give you their thoughtful feedback on a simple evaluation form that you have prepared for them.

PRESENTATION SKILLS	RATING (1–5; 5 BEING BEST)
Voice (volume, tone, vitality)	
Body language	
Eye contact with audience	
Humor	
Involving the audience	

INFORMATION PRESENTED	RATING
Well organized	
Clear and easy to follow	
Effective use of examples,	
statistics, quotations,	
anecdotes, support materials	
Value of ideas/information	

COMMENTS REGARDING STRENGTHS AND SUGGESTIONS FOR IMPROVEMENT:

_____

_____

_____

_____

4. Welcome Suggestions and Advice

Be sure to invite suggestions for improvement as much as you invite positive feedback. Of course we all love to hear positive remarks, but the comments for improvement are very helpful to our progress and ultimate success. Every time you present:

- Get feedback from others whose opinions you respect.
- Keep in mind that you have the right to disagree.
- Throw out the very worst evaluation you receive.
- Pay attention to similar comments when you hear them from several people.

- Remember what you did well and what worked so that you can repeat your successes.
- Think about what you will do differently next time.
- Be kind to yourself—it's human nature to be tough when evaluating your own performance.

5. Learn to Listen to and Evaluate Your Own Voice

How do you sound? At first, most people don't like to hear the sound of their own voices.

> Communication has become an art, but the key to being heard, listened to and liked is sound.
>
> —*Dr. Morton Cooper,* Winning with Your Voice

If you haven't done so recently, record yourself on audiotape and assess your vocal qualities. Do you hear energy, enthusiasm, and vitality in your voice? Can you hear a smile in your voice? If not, practice smiling each time you answer the phone and every time you walk into an office to meet with a client. When you're on the phone, 87 percent of your message is judged by the way you sound, and when you are face-to-face, it's 38 percent of your message. No one likes to listen to a monotone, or be distracted by a repetitive "uh," "er," or "um." (Dale Carnegie referred to these speech fillers as "word whiskers.")

If you don't like the sound of your own voice—and most people don't—here's my challenge to you: Change your voice mail message every day for 21 days. It takes 21 days to form a new habit and it takes just one to three minutes per day to change your phone message. In just three weeks, you will have a much greater awareness of your voice. And it will be a voice that I guarantee you'll like more than the one you have now.

6. Realize the Importance of Your Body Language

Body language sends our most powerful communication messages. Anytime our body language contradicts our words, people will believe our body language because it's five to 10 times more powerful than our verbal message. Videotaping yourself while practicing your presentations will help you to see if your body language is communicating the same message as your spoken one.

> Star quality happens when your inner strength matches your outer power and presence.
>
> —*Christen Brown*

Here are some examples of gestures that detract from your message and are best avoided:

1. Too much of anything: head nodding, fidgeting, quick gestures, or too many gestures
2. Nodding "yes" when you're saying "no"
3. Shaking your head "no" when you're saying "yes"
4. Closed or choppy gestures
5. Leaning to one side or putting more of your weight on one foot
6. Pointing or shaking your finger at another person
7. The "fig-leaf" posture (hands clasped in front, or in back, of your body)

Here are some pointers for enhancing your image and effectiveness as a presenter:

> Never bend your head. Always hold it high. Look the world straight in the face.
>
> —*Helen Keller,*
> *to a five-year-old blind child*

1. Keep your head straight when you're speaking
2. Distribute your weight evenly on both feet
3. Use open, palm-up gestures
4. Lean forward slightly when conversing and persuading
5. Hold your gestures for a second or two

6. Maintain eye contact for two to three seconds in order to really connect with your audience
7. Keep your hands and gestures at waist-level and above

7. Make Eye Contact for Greater Credibility

Be certain you have positive eye contact, because others will judge your credibility by it. When presenting, I've asked audiences, "What do you think of a person who doesn't have much eye contact with you?" Inevitably, I hear the following responses. "The person is lying, hiding something, dishonest, lacking confidence, or shy." I've never heard a positive comment about lack of eye contact.

> What you are not saying is definitely and clearly communicated.

When you connect with someone else, hold your eye contact for two to three seconds before looking elsewhere. To develop more positive eye contact, challenge yourself to look people in the eye when you speak to them. Make it a habit to say "hello" and establish eye contact first as you walk past someone in the hall or at a social event. The person who initiates the greeting is perceived as confident and as a leader—an added benefit.

8. Be Real, Be Genuine, Be You

After speaking at a televised national convention event, former first lady Barbara Bush was complimented on her speech by a news reporter. She quickly corrected the reporter by saying, "Oh, no, no. I wasn't giving a speech. I was just talking to people." Yes, just 20 to 30 million TV viewers and thousands of cheering conventioneers. Truthfully, she did sound as if she was "just talking to people." Her style was easy to listen to and comfortable, and it worked beautifully for getting her points across.

> I finally stopped running away from myself. Who else is there better to be?
>
> —Goldie Hawn

To genuinely connect with your audience, let them know you're there to give them something of value. To "sound real" and not arrogant, use common vocabulary. To "look real," breathe, smile, move naturally, and look into people's eyes. Show that you're enthusiastic about your topic. You will enjoy giving your presentation more than you ever imagined when you keep in mind that you're just talking to people.

9. Laugh and Project a Real Sense of Humor

Generating laughter from the start of your presentation will help to relax you and your audience, and you'll come across as a more confident person. Consider the Southwest Airlines flight attendant who grabbed his passengers' attention, made them sit up and want to hear more when he said, "There may

> I believe that humor is the bond that can unite us all.
>
> —*Ellie Marek*

be 50 ways to leave your lover, but there are only five ways to leave this airplane." The passengers not only heard his safety instructions, but they also visibly relaxed into laughter and acknowledged the flight attendant with a hearty round of applause.

Begin saving, recording, and filing humorous quotations, one-liners, true-life stories, anecdotes from famous people. Write down self-effacing humorous events from your life, then borrow from your file to add humor to your presentations.

Appropriate humor works because it connects people. Everyone loves to laugh, and if you can laugh at yourself, you're thought of as more confident and more likable. If you can laugh with a client, you'll probably do business with that client.

> Believe in yourself.

10. Organize Your Thoughts and Practice, Practice, Practice

To become your best you have to prepare, practice, and present. It's in the doing that you will learn. You'll feel much more confident if you learn to quickly organize your presentations. When given any topic, think of the main idea you want to get across to others, then break the problem, or issue, into three parts.

For example:

1. Problem
2. Solutions
3. Benefits

You can use a similar formula for any impromptu presentation. Here's a simple formula to use if you're called on to answer a question at a conference or during a meeting.

1. Restate the question
2. State your opinion
3. Give an example
4. Summarize

Remember that preparation before a meeting means that you've thought through, in advance, all of the questions that may come up. Mark Twain once said that it took him three weeks to prepare a good impromptu speech. In keeping with this tip, go into your meetings with that extra measure of preparation under your belt by anticipating audience questions and practicing your answers in advance.

Nothing can replace preparation and practice. Ninety percent of your confidence will come as a result of your advance work and rehearsals.

11. Dress the Part

While watching the evening news on a business trip to Hawaii, I was reminded of just how much more toughly society seems to judge women. A news reporter gave the results of a survey of voters' reactions to female political candidates. The report stated, "Voter reaction was 66 percent based on image and body language, 33 percent on voice, and 1 percent on what the candidate said." Like it or not, we are judged on the way we look, dress, stand, walk, and carry ourselves.

> Dress shabbily and people will remember the outfit. Dress elegantly and people will remember the person.
>
> *—Paraphrased from Coco Chanel*

When speaking, the general "rule of thumb" is this: always be as well dressed as the best-dressed person in your audience. This does not mean matching price tags or designer labels; it simply means that if people are wearing suits, so should you. Jackets are our most powerful pieces of clothing and will help any woman be perceived as having more authority.

12. Create a Self-Development and Educational Action Plan

If you don't like what you hear in your voice or you don't like what you see on video, you're probably ready to make some changes. If possible, hire a coach. You may also choose to practice your speaking skills through a college extension course on public speaking, a theater group, or a good Toastmasters club. Here are a number of resources.

> The future never just happened. It was created.
>
> *—Will and Ariel Durant*

> If you're willing to work, nothing is impossible.
>
> —*Oprah Winfrey*

Toastmasters International is the largest nonprofit, educational organization in the world, "dedicated to better speaking, thinking, listening, and leadership." Call your chamber of commerce for information regarding local clubs, or contact the Toastmasters World Headquarters at P.O. Box 9052, Mission Viejo, CA 92690.

For professionals wanting to expand and develop their speaking careers, contact the National Speakers Association (NSA), a professional organization "dedicated to advancing the art and the value of experts who speak professionally," at 1500 South Priest Dr., Tempe, AZ 85281, *www.nsaspeaker.org*.

For professionals in the training and human resource specialties, contact the American Society for Training and Development (ASTD). ASTD is the world's largest organization exclusively serving specialists in human resource development. ASTD, 1640 King Street, Box 1443, Alexandria, VA 22313.

Start Today

Start now to create the future you'd like to have by painting the portrait of the presenter and communicator you're capable of becoming. Be excited, prepared, polished, and professional. By doing so, you'll be reaching for the star in you. Get ready to shine and experience incredible success.

12 ACTION STEPS TO PRESENTATION AND COMMUNICATION SUCCESS

1. Know what you want to become.
2. Decide that you want to turn your fears into excitement. Say "yes" when you are invited to speak.
3. Evaluate yourself using audio and videotapes. Know what you like about your own communication and write out very specific goals for improvement.
4. Welcome feedback and advice from people whose opinions you trust. Get an objective evaluation by a professional coach.
5. Learn to listen to and evaluate your voice. Make time to take action and practice daily.
6. Realize the importance of your body language. Gestures and movements are five to 10 times more powerful than our words.
7. Project positive eye contact to increase your credibility.
8. Be genuine, be honest, and be you whenever you speak.
9. Include appropriate humor in your presentations, and be willing to laugh at yourself.
10. Organize your thoughts and practice, practice, practice. Never "wing it."
11. Dress the part. Project your best for greater self-assurance.
12. Create an ongoing self-development and educational action plan. Start today.

About the Author

Mary-Ellen Drummond, president of Polished Presentations International, is a full-time professional speaker, seminar leader, and consultant based in North San Diego County. She's the author of several books, including *Fearless and Flawless Public Speaking*. Her programs emphasize the power of enhancing presentation skills, communication, customer service, and personal excellence. Drummond's clients include *Fortune* 500 companies, sales organizations, health-care centers, and international associations. She has hosted her own radio talk show and is frequently interviewed by the media as she travels to more than 100 national and international engagements annually.

Mary-Ellen Drummond, President
Polished Presentations International
P.O. Box 2104
Rancho Santa Fe, CA 92067
Phone: (858) 756-4248 & (800) 728-9622
Fax: (858) 756-9621
E-mail: *medrummond@aol.com*
Web site: *www.medrummond.com*

chapter six

Professional Image Moxie: What Does Your Personal Style Say about You?

DIANE PARENTE
President, Image Development and Management, Inc.

Your image is talking even when you're not. As a professional, you can come in contact with hundreds of people every day—in meetings, at lunch, even traveling from place to place. You and your business may have all the substance in the world, but if you don't project a strong, professional image to go with it, people aren't going to respond the way you want them to.

I learned all this the hard way. As a child, I had little interest in clothes, but my indifference vanished as I prepared for my first day as a high school freshman. Now I had really grown up, and I wanted to make a big impression. I did, but not the kind I counted on.

My parents were blue-collar workers in a small town in Northern California where I grew up. There was never much money, but they instilled in their children a strong sense of personal pride and respect for others. All summer long before my freshman year, I planned what I would wear and do in my new adult role. Finally, my grandmother, Nanie, took me clothes shopping at J.C. Penney's. There we selected the three outfits that would last me through the school year. We spent hours carefully choosing just the right clothes.

The big day arrived. I got up early to bathe and iron my white Peter Pan blouse and floral-print skirt. I dressed, laced up my shoes, and took a long look in the mirror. The model of a high school freshman. Proudly, I arrived at school in my new outfit. But no one else was dressed like me. I stuck out like someone from another planet. I spent lunchtime and recess in the bathroom so I wouldn't see the stares or have to endure the giggles.

This traumatic experience taught me the importance of image and how your image can have a positive or negative influence on both yourself and others. For the first time, I began observing what others were wearing. Fortunately, my family moved to another school district the following summer, so I was able to start fresh with new schoolmates who hadn't pigeonholed me by my clothes. By then I had learned how to sew, and I made copies of the currently fashionable styles so I would blend right in. My classmates weren't put off by my exterior image, so they wanted to get to know the interior me. My self-esteem and confidence rose.

If this seems tremendously superficial, it is. But first impressions are sometimes all we have. If we don't click, we don't get a second chance. It is as true in the boardroom as it is in the classroom.

Your Public Package

Your public image represents the package of who you are and what you do. It's a reflection of your private self-image. When you portray yourself to the world as confident and competent, people respond more positively. The news divisions of KPIX-TV (CBS) and KRON-TV (NBC) in San Francisco secured my consulting services when they realized that most of their mail consisted of comments about the appearance of their news anchors. When these anchors followed my recommendations for enhancing their images, the ratings went up.

Of course, image can mask a lack of substance, but rarely for long. To back up your image, you also need a good product, extensive knowledge, and strong communications skills. Your image creates the expectation. Your substance confirms it.

Your ideal image should be so supportive of what you're saying that people can look past you to your message. We have all run into people whose appearance and actions are so distracting that we can't absorb their meaning. When we see a man with a bad hairpiece or an exotic combing over a bald spot, we wonder if he realizes how odd he looks. Or we notice a woman wearing a very short skirt. Will she be able to sit and still look professional? We become so engrossed in our own thoughts that we fail to hear their words.

> Nothing succeeds like the appearance of success.
>
> —*Christopher Leach*

How Style Changed My Life

It all started in 1977. The customer was standing with her arms full of clothes and her eyes full of doubt in the small boutique where I worked as a salesperson. "I just don't know if any of these outfits is right for me. Can you help me?" I responded with self-assurance and sent her out happy and enthusiastic. When she began sending her friends to me, I found myself embarked on a new career: image consulting.

Initially, I spent a great deal of time helping clients find the right palette for their personal wardrobes. I would drape them in colored bibs and produce color-fans for them to carry with them when they went shopping. From there I expanded into home wardrobe consultations, showing clients how to maximize their current wardrobe. This led to the next and most lucrative phase of my career, personal shopping. Clients appreciated shopping with me several times a year, knowing that they would look terrific and appropriate and convey a consistent image. The high level of repeat business quickly made this my main source of income.

Even with this early success I realized that, for my business to grow, I needed visibility. I moved to a posh office in a well known skin care salon in downtown San Francisco. Over the next 10 years, I saw a significant increase in my client list. I also broke into the network of business seminars.

At the first professional development seminar I ever attended, I found a dynamic Englishwoman working the gathering audience like a pro. The Emporium was sponsoring a series called "Tuesdays at 10," and she was the day's speaker. She walked up to me and said, "I'm Patricia Fripp. You look so terrific. You have to be somebody famous, but I don't recognize you." I laughed. "I'm not famous. I'm an image consultant." My outfit that day consisted of color-coordinated blouse, skirt, hat, and shoes in mauve.

Patricia Fripp introduced me to the Emporium marketing manager and insisted she hire me. This encounter ignited my career. The store invited me back to present image programs for their customers, and I began doing professional image seminars for audiences of all sizes, from small business groups to retail extravaganzas all over the United States. My clients came to include Amway Distributors, the American Payroll Association, the Hyatt Regency Hotel in San Francisco, Macy's of Northern California, the Ford Motor Company, and Corporate Property Investors.

Your Four Minutes

Leonard Zunin, author of *Contact: The First 4 Minutes*, says, "Four minutes is the average time demonstrated to grab someone's attention and establish credibility and rapport." Many of us decide even sooner. When you're making your way up the TV dial, how long do you pause at each channel to see if it engages you? In a world of quick sound bites and 30-second commercials, consumers can form opinions almost instantaneously. Your strong first impression is what gets you your four minutes.

Which Image?

Today, you have choices. That's both a powerful plus and a potential trap. Gone are the days of conservative clone outfits, dull but very safe. No more arcane rules about what can be worn with what and when. Now you can present the image that best projects you and your particular business. However, this

> Looking the part helps get you the chance to fill it.
>
> —*Malcolm Forbes*

new range of choices can be confusing, challenging, even frightening, and not without pitfalls. Should you go for the cutting-edge of fashion? Or the most conservative? Or something in between?

This depends on the culture of your industry, even within your industry. (When I did a workshop for PG&E, you could tell which floor people worked on by how they dressed.) "Business Casual" can be anything from a company-logo tee and artfully torn jeans to $1,200 silk separates. Do your homework.

And before you begrudge men the simplicity of their dressing choices, think again. Depending on the setting, a man's bow tie can indicate an original thinker or a dangerous nonconformist. An exact copy of the current "uniform" can indicate a team player or a mindless clone. Even the way his tie is knotted or his belt is buckled can signal that this person is clueless and "not one of us" or a member of a rival group. The subtle but specific messages characterized by gang colors and symbols pervade every profession and every level of society.

There is no one perfect image for a professional woman. The correct image for a rising star in the FBI will be very different from that of a corporate marketing director, a software sales rep, or a TV anchorwoman. And the clothes that were perfect 20 or even five years ago may not be today, just as your current styles can mark you as unobservant, boring, or overconservative years from now and be wildly inappropriate in 2020. Your challenge is to notice and understand your options.

The Seven Images

Over the past 20 years, I've analyzed the style of more than 5,000 clients and determined that they can be divided into seven basic images. Four are classic and three are nonclassic.

This unique model earned me an award for excellence from the Association of Image Consultants, and is described in one of my four coauthored books, *Mastering Your Professional Image*. Macy's hired me to teach this concept to their Northern California personal shoppers to help them better qualify and serve their clients. And I used this model when I was asked by KPIX-TV and the *San Francisco Chronicle* to analyze the clothing messages of the major "players" during the O. J. Simpson trial.

The Four Classics

Traditionals and Sportys are approachable and accessible styles. Both blend in with the group, creating a low profile for the wearer. These styles are ideal for those who want to appear friendly and easygoing, not overpowering.

Elegants and Dramatics stand out as leaders, women who want to create a high profile. These styles are especially good for those who want to be taken more seriously in the business world and for those who must correct misperceptions of inexperience because they are petite or appear extremely young.

The world is governed more by appearances than realities.

—*Daniel Webster*

TRADITIONAL

This is the most recognized way to dress for business. It communicates that you are a supportive and conscientious team player who conforms to established standards and doesn't want to stand out. Traditional is often called "mainstream." The look is conservative and neat, relying on blazer-style suits and coat-dresses. Open a Traditional's closet and you will see the same outfit in a myriad of menswear neutrals.

You are the message.

Preferred by: Those in finance, government, law, or news-casting who want to blend in and resemble seasoned East Coast professionals.

SPORTY

Because of the recent growth in popularity of Business Casual, this has become the most common way to dress in business today. Functional Sporty communicates that you are an approachable team player with a candid and open personality, someone who is friendly and prefers lots of activity. The look is youthful, unstudied, and slightly tousled, usually a combo of traditional and active sportswear, but more casual and colorful. Shirts are unbuttoned at the neck, jackets are left open, and sleeves may be pushed up. Comfortable mix-and-match coordinates are the norm.

Preferred by: Professionals in sales, high-tech areas, academia, child-related services, the food industry, or medical fields who require stress-free dressing.

ELEGANT

A leadership style indicating a calm, cool, authority figure who is analytical, preferring structure and order, but with a bit more dash than the Traditional. It is characterized by refined taste and beauty. Favored by the perfectionist or well organized individual. The Elegant is understated, impeccably groomed from head to toe, and perfectly coordinated. The designs are streamlined, emphasizing beautiful fabrics, subtle colors, and perfect fit. Often there are couture details such as bound buttonholes, handsewn hems, hand-picking around lapels, and buttons matching the outfit.

Preferred by: Those wanting to emphasize the dignity of their positions and their firm control of the situation. Calm, cool authority figures who are discreetly declaring that they can handle anything without getting flustered.

DRAMATIC

Originating in high fashion and now worn by those seeking or in high positions. Often called "Statement Dressing," this one-of-a-kind look is striking and sophisticated. It generally uses an element of exaggeration such as wide shoulders, asymmetrical neckline, strong color contrasts, or bold accessories. Perfect grooming is an integral element of the Dramatic style. A current Dramatic look is a long suit jacket over a short skirt or a slim pair of pants.

Preferred by: Those wishing to demonstrate a commanding presence, communicating their assertiveness and independence. Favored by successful political figures, the entertainment industry, and those who run their own companies.

The Nonclassics

Nonclassics are appropriate for less conventional business situations unless combined with one of the four Classic styles.

ALLURING

Sexy, glamorous styles, inappropriate for most business situations. Alluring undermines credibility, but can be effective in some professions.

Preferred by: Those in the fitness and entertainment industries, nightclubs, bars, restaurants, casinos, etc.

FEMININE

Gentle, romantic, and ladylike, indicating softness, warmth, compassion. Does not project the forcefulness and assertiveness needed for most business situations. Its nonthreatening characteristic can help you bond with others.

Preferred by: Those doing direct home sales, providing therapy, or teaching elementary school.

CREATIVE

Imaginative and flamboyant. The Creative projects individual flair through unusual colors, textures, patterns, or designs. Effective for situations where you need to shout, "Notice me!"

Appropriate for: Those involved in fashion, cosmetology, and entertainment.

Clients tell me that understanding the seven images is an invaluable guide for planning and investing in their wardrobes.

My Turning Point

Soon after my most recent book was published, an Amway Executive Diamond hired me to present a seminar on the four classic business styles to her 2,000 distributors at a leadership conference in Washington, D.C. I was both delighted and dismayed: delighted because this would be my first really big speaking assignment and dismayed because I wasn't sure I could pull it off. But in the back of my mind, I kept hearing the voice of my dear friend and mentor, Patricia Fripp: "Go for it! Life is a series of learning experiences, and you must constantly challenge yourself to move forward."

> Our self-image and our habits tend to go together. Change one and you will automatically change the other.

There was less than a month to design the seminar and create the slides and handout materials. I worked night and day. One of my big decisions was to use women in the audience to illustrate how to maximize your image. After interviewing the volunteers about their personal and professional goals, I selected three for a makeover. Each received a new outfit, hairstyle, and makeup. "Before" and "after" slides were taken by a professional photographer to document the process.

On the big day, suffering from butterflies and the aftereffects of insomnia, I confronted 4,000 curious eyes. "This is big time!" I thought. "Now, show your stuff."

Everything went perfectly until I got to the slides. For the longest 10 minutes of my life, I struggled with one slide carousel that advanced forward while the second showed slides backward. Finally, I got them synchronized.

As an Elegant controlling type, I was devastated by my failure. As soon as the program was over, I snuck back to my book display in the lobby, sure they'd never invite me back. To my amazement, 300 women were already in line. For the next six hours, I signed copies of my book and offered miniconsultations on enhancing their appearance.

As a result of this success, I was immediately hired to present similar seminars in other locations and booked to return to the next conference in Washington, D.C. Every year since, I have consulted and done personal shopping for their top achievers, women from London to Beverly Hills. This one incredible experience generated book sales, seminars, consultations, and personal shopping business, teaching me the value of taking on new projects.

On a personal level, I also learned the importance of giving more than is expected and of doing business with women who share similar values. We can all overcome fear by confronting our challenges head-on. Perfection is less important than being real and open. Seek out friends who will support, nurture, and coach you, and be sure to do the same for them. Finally, enjoy what you are doing and have fun!

Saving the Situation

What if you've done your homework, but find yourself facing someone dressed very differently from you? If your client is very casual and you're in a suit, you can still save the day. Take off the jacket, or at least unbutton it and push up the sleeves. As surreptitiously as possible, open a shirt button or two, remove accessories, roll up shirt sleeves. On the other hand, if you're in jeans and your client is dressed for an audience with the pope, neaten yourself up as much as possible and depend on a formal, reserved, and respectful manner to carry off the occasion. How you carry yourself can make all the difference. (Once the actress Sarah Bernhardt was about to play her famous death scene from *The Lady of the Camellias*. No one could find the mandatory flower prop, so a stagehand offered a substitute. She died so exquisitely that no one in the audience noticed she was clutching a stick of celery from the man's lunch box. That's image moxie!)

Talking Behind Your Back

Your image can smooth your way or stop you cold. With great effort, you can usually overcome a bad first impression, but why waste the time? Start right, start strong, and your image will be your most powerful advocate, telling people who and what you are as you connect with them and get your message across. Professional image moxie boosts your credibility, inspires trust and confidence, and lets you face the world with assurance and zest.

8 Action Steps
for Professional Image Moxie

1. **Notice.** What do the stars in your chosen career niche wear? How do their superiors, colleagues, and customers respond to the way they dress? What can you learn from them—to do and *not* to do? What geographical or cultural differences can dictate altering your image if your job involves traveling? Would you do better to compete with or complement the people you want to impress?

2. **Assess.** Know yourself. What current styles and colors are most flattering to you? Have you been dressing "too young" or "too old"? Too conservative or too casual? Which styles will support the professional image you want to project? Which fit into your budget, workday, and lifestyle?

3. **Adapt.** Different situations demand different looks. Delivering a presentation to an important client may require the All-Out Power Look. Leading the group planning session calls for a more relaxed look. Calling on a high-tech client may require Business Casual. Do you want all eyes on you? Or should the product or someone else be the center of attention?

4. **Individualize.** Find a trademark that shows you know and care about how you look. For some women, this means always wearing a hat. For others, a signature color, handbag, or piece of jewelry. Even if your choices are severely restricted by your job description, you can still find ways to stand out. Have the shiniest polish on your shoes, the sharpest press on your clothes, the best-groomed hair and makeup.

5. **Invest.** You've planned your career strategy. Now plan how to acquire and maintain your ideal image without spending a fortune. Budget for the best quality you can afford on the pieces that matter. Skimp where it won't

show. Then make the daily effort to be what our grandmothers called "well turned-out." Maintain your wardrobe with the same dedication you'd maintain a luxury car, and it will carry you far, reinforcing and boosting your professional image as you go in style.

6. **Organize.** Don't waste time making decisions each morning. Get your closets, both physical and mental, in order. Accessories that can do double duty are nice as long as they are not *blah* wherever you use them. Find the perfect blouse, jewelry, or scarf for each outfit. You can even keep them on the same hanger—then you're not reinventing the wheel just when you need to get out the door fast. Keep your closet and dressing area as a staging area for maximum morning lift-off. Be merciless about weeding out that great sale item that never worked and the clothes you've outgrown, physically or professionally.

7. **Shop smart.** Keep color swatches or guidelines in your purse to avoid impractical impulse buying.

8. **Consult.** If you're being promoted, changing careers, or just need an image boost, and you're unsure how to proceed, consider getting advice from a professional. An unbiased observer can often give you new insights about your best looks and proportions as well as what works best in your industry. Just because you've always worn things a certain way doesn't mean it's best for you. An investment in professional image expertise can be invaluable to your professional future.

About the Author

Diane Parente is a pioneer and true visionary in the image industry. In the late 1970s, she became one of the first image consultants and personal shoppers. In 1984, she founded and was the first president of the Association of Image Consultants International, which now has chapters throughout the world. Today, Diane is president of Image Development and Management, Inc., a firm serving individuals and corporations who want to present a professional image that best sells their value. She is the coauthor of four books on style, the most recent *Mastering Your Professional Image*: *Dressing to Enhance Your Credibility*.

Diane Parente, President
Image Development and Management, Inc. (IDMI)
P.O. Box 262
Ross, CA 94957
Phone: (415) 258-0285
Fax: (415) 485-1793
Web site: *www.imagesellsyou.com*

chapter seven

Business Protocol

MARIE BETTS-JOHNSON
President, International Protocol Institute of California

Life is like an archaeological dig. The more you dig the more you find, the more you find, the more excited you become about searching further!

I believe we are most fortunate when we hear life asking us to search deep within and follow what feels right to us. We must never lose the courage to follow our dreams, because without dreams life would be hopeless. Who knows what's in store for us—reality may even surpass our dreams.

We are all born with unique gifts and talents. I believe that it is our duty to search for them and present them to the world. Some of us are born into

> As soon as you trust
> yourself you will know
> how to live.
>
> —*Goethe*

an area or location in the world that supports our life's passage. But there are those of us who must search until we find that place, whether it be country, state, or town, that feels most like home to our hearts. In our search for our true home, we may at times feel rudderless. But we can pick up crucial life skills at every step along the way. These skills, I know, can help us call forth our unique gifts and talents. I know because that's how it happened for me.

Listen and Follow Your Inner Drum

Growing up in an extremely conservative Catholic environment in Ireland, I had two choices—conform or leave. As extreme as it sounds, I chose the latter and I have never, for one moment, regretted my choice. It took courage and blind belief that there was much more out there to be explored in the world. I was not disappointed!

"The imagination is a wonderful thing—anyone should have one," said Oscar Wilde. Thankfully, I always had quite a vivid imagination! In Ireland, my first job was in a bank. This was a good, solid, pensionable job ("solid" being the operative word), but certainly not a job where imagination was particularly prized. Consequently, I took what would be considered in Ireland at that time a giant leap of faith or foolhardiness, and departed to "browner pastures," i.e., Amman, Jordan.

Jordan could not have been more different in every way. But, I was determined to make it work. With the "luck of the Irish" on my side, I became a member of the staff of King Hussein and Queen Noor of Jordan. It was in this enviable position that I had the opportunity to be a voyeur on the periphery of life. I observed everything from the lives of the painfully poor to those of the fabulously rich and concluded that wealth is everything and yet nothing. We all, as humans, have the same basic need for respect. The greatest lesson that I learned, and the one that has propelled me to this day in my profession, was seeing, firsthand, how His

Majesty King Hussein of Jordan brought people together through his extraordinary love, humility, and genuine passion for peace in his land.

After four years with Their Majesties, I came back to reality and came to the only country where people can be whatever they *imagine* they can be *if they work at it*—the United States of America. Having had the opportunity to explore most of the rest of the world, my intuition told me that this was it for me. Again, the United States was a culture shock, and I spent two years in San Francisco studying marketing and merchandising. This was but an exit on the freeway of my life, but the marketing knowledge that I attained *was* and *is* invaluable to me to this very day.

> Who needs a book of etiquette? Everyone does . . . for we must all learn socially acceptable ways of living.
>
> —*Amy Vanderbilt*

My next stop was San Diego, California. I began to use my fashion/marketing expertise as an "image consultant." It was extremely rewarding to witness the transformation that a new and complementary wardrobe could afford my clients. Yet it was clear to me that there was so much more needed to round off the entire package. And at once I knew that I was being called forward to provide that. All my travels on the highways and byways of life—which had taken me from Ireland to the Middle East to the United States, and many places in between—had brought me right to this point. I was being asked to draw on the skills I had learned, my in-depth experience of different cultures and the meetings between cultures, and my special gifts and talents to provide the missing pieces of the package for business professionals in this country.

The Complete Packaging

As companies and their products need a cohesive package and image to present a favorable impression to their consumers, professionals must also be packaged to create a credible impression in the minds of their discerning clients. In other words, it does not matter how wonderful our products or services are if we do not look and act the part! To be a truly polished professional, we must be able to handle any situation—business or social—with ease and confidence. It is wonderful if one is in great shape and one's "Armani" suit is impeccable, but that is but the icing on the cake. The cake itself must have all the right ingredients to be successful. Only when we have all the right ingredients do we have the complete packaging.

Business Etiquette

Business etiquette is the key to confidence. It is absolutely unbelievable how many so-called professionals I have come in contact with who do not know how to handle everyday introductions or shake hands with confidence. Their business cards are a sorry crumpled mess stuck deep in their pockets. They hand their business cards out to anyone who is unfortunate enough to look their way. Their eye contact is anywhere but where it should be—on the person they are speaking to. They attend one networking meeting after another having no idea how to make a true connection with people. They view these social forays as a necessary means to meet potential clients, but forget that clients are *people first, not meal tickets*, and that they deserve respect. We respect people through knowledge of etiquette and making them feel valuable. Next time you attend a meeting consider that most of us cannot remember the names of the people we have been introduced to because we are too busy thinking of something else!

My personal philosophy is to arrive at a meeting early before each presentation. My host usually introduces me to as many people as possible or, if the host is busy, I will introduce myself. I give the person I am conversing with my undivided attention— not my business card—until they request it. Because I strive to truly listen to what they have to say, they sometimes openly share their protocol faux pas with me then and there. Later, during my speech, they may enhance my presentation by sharing their protocol mishaps again with the audience. These *initial* strangers become friendly faces in my audience because we have shared some personal experiences. They sense that I am genuinely interested in what they have to share with me. To make a real connection, I recommend spending at least 10 minutes with each person you meet. Do not be in too great a rush to meet every person in the room. Make a true human connection!

> Protocol is about rank and order and etiquette is about putting others at ease with you and conducting yourself in a non-offensive manner.
>
> —*Gloria Petersen*

Make an Entrance

Many business professionals show their lack of confidence by walking into a room full of potential business contacts with shoulders slumped and a glum expression on their faces. They view networking situations as a zoo at feeding time by making a mad dash for the hors d'oeuvres. Their conversation is reduced to disjointed mumblings in between mouthfuls of food. They lose the power of the handshake, which is the only acceptable greeting in business, because they cannot possibly hold a glass in one hand and a plate in the other and still shake hands. Furthermore, their mouths are otherwise engaged and, in truth, they are totally incapacitated!

Dining Etiquette

> *The world was my oyster, but I used the wrong fork.*
>
> —OSCAR WILDE

Dining etiquette is one's passport to confidence in both social and business situations. I have seen extremely accomplished professionals, from every walk of life, literally stab their food with their forks, talk with their mouths full, blow their noses with their napkins, use the wrong utensil for the course being served, drink from their finger bowls, and more.

Recently, I made a presentation on international protocol to a prestigious group of business people. I omitted mentioning any-thing about the mechanics of using the proper knife and fork, assuming they would have perfect table manners, and was surprised when a former chief of protocol in the audience asked me to explain this aspect of etiquette to the audience. Of course, I was happy to do so, and later I asked him why he made this request. He told me that the person who was sitting next to him had such deplorable table manners that he thought it would be beneficial if I demonstrated some vital pointers on basic dining etiquette before this gentleman ventured overseas to conduct business!

I cannot help feeling embarrassed for all the poor souls who are unaware of the impression they are creating. To be a well rounded professional in any business, we must have all the tools of the trade. It is such a waste of energy to have to worry about which fork to use when we are trying to conclude an important business deal. The sad fact is that many busy parents are either unaware of etiquette rules themselves, or they do not have time to teach their children the fundamentals of dining etiquette. If this is a dilemma, I strongly suggest buying one of the many excellent books on the subject or attending a business etiquette seminar in your local area as soon as possible!

Globalization

The world is here—it's not over there. At no other time in history has there been such an opportunity to interact with and conduct business with people from so many diverse backgrounds and cul-tures both at home and abroad. When we first find our passion, we tend to spend our time perfecting our products and services. Our second concern must be to research the culture, protocol, and eti-quette of our potential clients. (Opportunities overseas abound.) But, to be successful, we must thoroughly understand the intricacies of their religions, philosophies, cultural variables, and, of course, their protocol and etiquette norms, in order to best understand how we can meet their needs. Most importantly, when they see that we have taken the time to understand their norms, they know that we respect them as people.

For instance, it would not be a good idea to attempt to sell dairy products to Asians, who for the most part are lactose intolerant, or to present a car with the steering wheel on the left to the Irish or Japanese, who drive on the left-hand side of the road. Millions of dollars are lost every year by U.S. companies who do not take the time for, or see the importance of, adequately researching their potential markets.

Getting the Word Out about Your Business

The best promotion for my business was writing a monthly article for the local business journal. I still get calls, four years later, from people who saved my articles. We can also get extra mileage from our articles by putting them on the Internet and including them in our public relations packets. Writing articles positions us in the marketplace as the expert in our particular fields. Advertising our goods and services is also quite effective. It is a good idea to establish a relationship with the editor of the publication, who may find the topic so interesting that he or she decides to do a feature article to accompany the advertisement.

> Family and friends are like the pillars on the porch. Sometimes they hold you up, and sometimes they lean on you. Sometimes it's just enough to know they're standing by.
>
> **—Anonymous**

Speak, Speak, Speak

Many of us have had great ideas and are not capable of getting them across because of weak presentation skills. When I started out in my business, I was extremely shy and speaking in public was excruciating for me. My first stop was Toastmasters International, which provided an invaluable, supremely supportive "nuts 'n bolts" training ground to overcome my many speaking gaffes! From there, I graduated to the National Speakers Association, which, along with adding to my presentation skills, provided extensive information on how to run a business as a speaker and a trainer. It also provided a network of professionals who had in the past, and were currently, encountering the same challenges as I was, and this was a tremendous support when I was making my debut. The final step is to polish our act! To do this, I sought out a person whom I admire and respect to help me hone my skills. I chose the author of this book, Mary-Ellen Drummond, who was well up to the task as my personal coach.

> You must do the things you think you cannot do.
>
> —*Eleanor Roosevelt*

Family and Friends

"Keep the home fires burning." Let's not lose sight of the truly important things in life—family and friends. As my star was beginning to rise, I noticed that my little boy was having difficulties at school. The more I worried about him, the less I could concentrate on my work. After playing tug-of-war between my business and professional life for many months, I decided, since he is my first priority, to give him my full attention and get to the bottom of the problem. After two years, a solution was found and everything worked out fine.

Taking time out for my family also had an unexpected outcome. Because each life experience gives us new insights into who we are and what is truly important, I returned to my career with a totally new perspective and sense of purpose. After going through this very difficult period, I found that I no longer fear making presentations. The perspective I've gained has given me a new confidence when connecting with my audiences.

Friends are our lifeline. As we all know, good friends are hard to find, but when we find them, we must also take the time to nurture these relationships. Everybody is rushing around in a million directions these days, and sometimes our friendships fall by the wayside. Friends are there to share in the good times as well as the bad and can often offer a completely different perspective on life's more perplexing challenges. In this society, "time is money." I agree, but I would like to add, "Time is money, but friends are priceless."

Pooling Your Talents

As entrepreneurs we must wear many hats. We fill the roles of president of the company, marketing/financial director, research and development specialist, and office manager. This is where past experiences are invaluable. For once, age is an asset when embarking on a new career or profession. With age comes experience. In my case, my experience for my profession as an international protocol expert came from working in a bank (office expertise), interacting with diverse global dignitaries and royalty (protocol experience and human relations skills), marketing and merchandising studies (marketing and public relations expertise), and Toastmasters International and the National Speakers Association (presentation skills).

Take It Easy on Yourself

I know it's a jungle out there. It seems like such a cliché to suggest that when we fall down we must pick ourselves up and dust ourselves off. But that is exactly what needs to be done. There will always be the temptation to compare ourselves with others who are better presenters or who have more financial success. But, we must follow our own path even if it means taking some blind leaps of faith or taking a step backward to redirect our energies on the right path. May you enjoy your archaeological dig. Keep searching!

Final Words of Wisdom

- **Listen and follow your inner drum.** It is our duty—and privilege—to search for our unique gifts and talents, to find our passion, to follow our dreams, and to present them to the world.
- **Packaging.** We must present a cohesive package. The outside must be congruent with the inside.
- **Business etiquette/international protocol.** Etiquette in all its forms gives us the confidence to handle any situation with polish and finesse. It also gives us the tools to be gracious human beings capable of exhibiting respect for ourselves and others both at home and overseas.
- **Make an entrance.** What the heck! You only live once. Stand up and be counted. You're entitled.
- **Dining etiquette.** If we wish to continue to live in a civilized society, then civility in all things must reign. Dining situations open the door to establishing friendships and business relationships. Dining etiquette came about because it was the most civilized, logical way to eat and enjoy good food while concentrating on the important business of getting to know each other.
- **Globalization.** The world is here; it is not over there. We may enjoy the similarities, but we must learn about others and our differences in order to show true respect.
- **Getting the word out.** Many of us have wonderful ideas at night just before we go to sleep. Jot them down. Then use them as seed materials for articles.
- **Speak, speak, speak.** No matter what business we choose, we must be capable of articulating our concepts to others, be they individuals or groups. Our verbal message represents our business; therefore, our message must be strong, powerful, and thoroughly polished.

- **Family and friends.** Life sticks out its foot once in a while to trip us up and teach us a new lesson. Without supportive relationships, we may have a difficult time experiencing and growing beyond the lesson to meet the inevitability of life's next hurdle.
- **Pooling your talents.** Sometimes we may not realize how many talents we bring to the table. Whenever we take on a task that is outside of our comfort zone we can use it as an opportunity to identify the many talents we have pooled together to follow our passion.
- **Take it easy on yourself.** Most entrepreneurs are, by their very nature, perfectionistic. Simply being aware of this quality in ourselves will help us keep it in perspective.

About the Author

Marie Betts-Johnson, founder and president of the International Protocol Institute of California, is an internationally recognized consultant, speaker, and columnist. She has developed hundreds of customized training programs for top U.S. corporations, including IBM, Gucci Timepieces, Sony Corporation, W-D 40 Company, and the International Bankers' Association of California. Based in San Diego since 1989, Ms. Betts-Johnson provides cross-cultural briefings for individuals who are relocating abroad and those who are coming to the United States for the first time. She is well known for her work as protocol coordinator for the Diplomatic Corps of the 1996 Republican National Convention. Her work outside the United States included four years on the staff of King Hussein and Queen Noor of Jordan. Her protocol assignments included Prince Charles and the late Princess Diana of Wales, King Juan Carlos of Spain, and United States Secretary of State George Schultz.

Marie Betts-Johnson, President
International Protocol Institute of California
P.O. Box 676147
Rancho Santa Fe, CA 92067
Phone: (858) 259-8302
Fax: (858) 259-9650
E-mail: *MBJProtocl@aol.com*

chapter eight

Speaking the Language of Success

JULIE WHITE, PH.D.
President, Julie White & Associates

One of my clients, a major brokerage firm, had a problem. The firm had brought together five of their top financial consultants for a panel discussion to analyze the market and to predict future trends. After videotaping the discussion, the firm sent out the tape as a special perk to their top clients across the country. It seemed like an excellent marketing idea, designed to give an insider's view of the market to their very best customers.

Management was flabbergasted, however, when female customers began calling the firm to say, "If this is the way you treat women in your organization, I'm taking my business elsewhere!" What had happened? The panel had consisted of four men and one woman, all equally qualified. As the woman explained to me, "After the initial introductions, I never got

> What women want is what men want. They want respect.
>
> —*Marilyn vos Savant*

another word in edgewise. I never got another chance to speak." The woman, of course, had been acutely aware that she hadn't been able to contribute to the discussion. But everyone else, from the producer to the director to the videographers to the staff in the marketing department, had never even noticed until the negative feedback came rolling in. Long after the event, the woman was still genuinely hurt and offended. As she explained to me, "I honestly thought the other guys respected me and my track record. It was an unpleasant shock to realize they didn't respect me after all."

As a communications consultant and trainer, I often get to hear "inside stories" like this one; most corporations don't publicize their mistakes to the general public. When they called me in to the organization to help fix the problem, I explained that the issue hadn't been sexism, despite what the outraged clients had claimed, or any lack of respect from the male panelists, despite what the lone woman had felt. What had happened was a classic conflict of two different cultures—two "Gender Cultures," each viewing the world and speaking about it differently.

Since we are all blind to our own Gender Culture (it's the old fish-in-water thing), we often have no idea of what is really going on with the opposite sex. In this

> The world cares very little about what a man or woman knows; it is what the man or woman is able to do that counts.
>
> —*Booker T. Washington*

chapter, I want to discuss a few of the most important differences between male and female culture, and illustrate how those differences get communicated through our gender-specific speech. Different cultures aren't better or worse than other cultures. But cultural norms—accepted cultural behavior—can be strikingly different from what we expect to encounter, as our female panelist found out.

When in Rome . . .

If we were to travel to another country and find that the customs and ceremonies, the conversational rituals and interpersonal behaviors seemed a bit strange, we wouldn't automatically judge the inhabitants of that country or immediately assume that their treatment of us was disrespectful. Before traveling to a foreign land, we realize that it's a good idea to learn a few words and phrases in their language, to brush up on that country's social etiquette, and to learn some of what is expected of us. But when women and men encounter a different Gender Culture, right here at home among our colleagues, our friends, and our relatives, we often attribute misunderstandings not to a different culture, but rather to an inappropriate or elitist attitude. Our tendency is to jump to more stereotyping and negative assumptions: "I realized they didn't really respect me after all." "You can't trust them to keep a secret." "You know how she got that new promotion, don't you?" "They're only after one thing."

Conversation Is Governed by Rituals

Much of our communication is governed by conversational rituals, commonly understood ways of speaking. As North Americans, we commonly greet people with "How are ya?" and we all know that this is a ritual utterance, not a genuine question. We are not really inquiring about the other person's health; we just want to hear, "Fine, thanks." In the culture of Mozambique, the greeting ritual is, "Have you eaten?" In which case, the answer is always, "Yes." In Indonesia, "Where are you going?" gets the appropriate answer, "Over there." When we are not aware of the ritual nature of conversation, we make the mistake of taking the words literally. Anyone who heard, "How

> [Women] are bridging the gap and proving that not only do we have something worthwhile to say—we are saying things that bear repeating.
>
> —*Erma Bombeck*

are ya?" literally, and started to discuss their sinus problem, would be quickly shunned.

While traveling in Southeast Asia, I was surprised to learn that Americans are often seen as superficial and uncaring. Why? "They ask how you are, and then they don't even bother to listen to your answer." In Bali, I was scared to death walking on a lonely beach, when I suddenly found myself surrounded by a group of five Balinese men. While perfectly pleasant, they kept asking me, "Where are you going? Where are you going?" With American sexual assault statistics whirling in my head, I kept thinking, "What do they want? Why do they want to know?" I wish I had known the ritual nature of the question, and that the ritual response was simply "Over there."

Women's Ways of Speaking

Imagine a group of women having lunch and talking together. What conversational rituals will you hear? Women in all-women groups use "turn-taking" as a way of changing the speaker. In fact, if another woman hasn't used her turn, we'll point it out to her, "Marge, you've been quiet today. What's your view on this?" Women try to be fair in the amount of "airtime" they take. One woman can certainly be more talkative than the rest, but in general, women unconsciously calculate, "Now let's see, there's five of us here, I'll talk about 20 percent of the time." When a woman uses much more airtime than her share, she apologizes or at least feels uncomfortable, "I'm sorry. I've gone on and on about this. . . ."

> Men are taught to apologize for their weaknesses, women for their strengths.
>
> —*Lois Wyse*

Our group of women at lunch would use supportive talk: "Marge, you're good at this, you've dealt with this before, so what do you think?" Women often pause once they've finished a thought, to give the listener a chance to jump into the conversation with her comments. And, although we all sometimes interrupt and overlap the conversation, women have been taught to see interruption as "rude."

Most important, our women talking at lunch would have used their speech as a way of maintaining equal status, or at least the appearance of equality. A woman will often downplay her expertise to maintain that appearance of equality. You could hear that all-important equal status in conversations like, "Marge, you did a great job giving that presentation. I was really impressed." "Well, thanks, Jane. Your view of the situation was particularly insightful."

What just happened here? When Marge got complimented on her great presentation, she became, however temporarily, "one up." To restore that all-important sense of equality, she brought Jane up to the same level. Marge's compliment to Jane says, "I'm not the only one who can do a good job; you did also." There's another way Marge could have restored equality—by moving herself, however subtly, back down to Jane's level. You hear this one all the time, "Thanks, Jane. But to tell you the truth, I was scared to death when I got up to speak." Once again, the appearance of equality is maintained. Women learn as young girls that flaunting their expertise elicits a "Who does she think she is?" response, and so women learn to downplay their expertise by emphasizing the similarities between themselves and the listener.

> Women are still fighting for credibility.
>
> —*Robin Roberts*

Women in all-women groups use speech to show connection and support, to reach consensus, and to simply enjoy the conversation. They use turn-taking, share "airtime," and maintain at least the appearance of equality. Our female stockbroker, participating in the panel discussion, expected to play by these rules.

Men's Ways of Speaking

Our four male stockbrokers were playing by an entirely different set of rules. Men in all-male groups have a very different view of the rules of conversation. Men tend to use conversation as a negotiation for status, where they try to achieve or maintain the upper hand. If they can't be "top dog," they at least protect themselves from another man's attempts to put them down. "John, get me a beer while you're up." "Get it yourself. What do you think I am, your wife?" You would recognize an all-male group out at lunch by this kind of verbal banter, their good-natured put-downs, and the rough-and-tumble nature of their conversation in which no one waits to be called on, but simply jumps into the verbal fray.

Far from turn-taking or unconsciously calculating how much airtime is their "fair share," men prove the worth of their ideas by holding the floor. If they give up too easily, other men may assume they're unsure of, or uncommitted to, their own ideas. How good can an idea be if the originator himself is unwilling to fight for it? The men on the panel used interruption and overlap as their method of changing speakers. Pointing out to another man that he hasn't used his "turn" would be considered insulting. As a man in my "Gender Trap: Men and Women Working Together" seminar explained, "What do you want me to do? Send him an engraved invitation? He's a big boy. He can take care of himself."

Comfortable with using conversation as a method of achieving or maintaining the upper hand, the men jumped into the conversation to get their ideas heard, even if another man hadn't quite finished talking. These were the invisible rules the four male panelists were using in their panel discussion.

The woman, waiting her turn to speak, found that her turn never came. Waiting for others to finish and pause to give her a chance to speak, she never spoke at all. No one was right or wrong, good or bad, here. The invisible rules of each Gender Culture were determining how each person spoke. It was as if one of the panelists were speaking a foreign language, and no one realized the problem.

What Can Women Do?

Having led hundreds of workshops for women ranging from trial attorneys to postal workers, nursing supervisors to financial professionals, I hear the same complaint time and time again: "I'm good at what I do, I work harder than anyone else in my department, I get along with everyone else on the staff. So, why am I passed over for promotions, prestige assignments, a shot at the top?" "Why can't I get a word in edgewise at important meetings?" "Why, when I make a point, does no one take it seriously, yet when a male colleague makes the same point, he gets everyone's attention?"

Most often, these women are not victims of outright sexism. The problem I see is that these women are using common female speech patterns that work well in all-female groups but that make them seem less confident and unsure of themselves in male eyes. Once women begin to understand the other Gender Culture and change their way of talking to match the dominant culture, they finally start getting the respect and airtime they deserve. A librarian from Toronto wrote me this after taking my "Language of Success" course.

> *Two days ago, I had a difficult meeting with my boss, and for the VERY FIRST TIME IN NINE YEARS, I was pleased with the outcome. At the end of the 45 minute volley, my heart wasn't pounding, my face wasn't flushed, and my chest wasn't tight from stress.*

Verbal Sabotage

Women often sabotage their own good ideas. In my seminars, when I go over the list of the ways in which women sound ineffective, I can almost hear the women participants saying to themselves, "Julie, *we* don't do that." Then I pass out a set of difficult, one-sentence statements. They range from terminating another's employment to asking for a

> Whether women are better than men I cannot say—but I can say they are certainly no worse.
>
> —*Golda Meir*

25 percent salary increase. In pairs, each woman delivers the statements to her partner. The partner's job is to give the speaker honest feedback on how she comes across, and not to let her move on to the next statement until she's believable. Suddenly, self-sabotaging patterns become crystal clear.

As I walk around the room, I see women "terminating employment" with appeasing half-smiles on their faces. They ask for a 25 percent salary increase with a lilting, upward inflection and a pleading little girl tilt to their head. They look away on the difficult word, signaling loud and clear their discomfort with what they are saying. Their partners "get it" immediately and work hard to help them come across with credibility. Often the partners can't tell exactly what the speaker is doing wrong, but they understand clearly that the message isn't coming through. It's a valuable exercise, and one I would recommend to all women.

> Some questions don't have answers, which is a terribly difficult lesson to learn.
>
> —*Katherine Graham*

Although most women sabotage their effectiveness by coming across as too weak, I also encounter a smaller group of women who have swung the pendulum too far in the other direction. They bark out orders, coming across not strong, but tough, almost as if they expect the listener to disagree and give them a hard time.

Keep in mind there is never a "right" or "wrong" way to communicate. The question to ask yourself is always: "Is what I'm doing working?"

Here are seven of the most common verbal sabotage patterns I've heard over the years. You may not do all of them, but it is a safe bet that you need to change at least one or two.

1. HEDGING YOUR BETS

- "This may not be important, but . . ."
- "I guess my question is . . ."
- "I hate to bring this up, but . . ."
- "John, I was just wondering if . . ."

Starting a sentence with any of these sorts of hedge phrases is a typical female way of speaking. Their intention is to soften whatever additional information the speaker is about to give. As a part of women's inclusive way of speaking, there is nothing inherently wrong with using hedge phrases. In fact, if you are delivering unpleasant or bad news, hedge phrases can be useful.

I once had a male boss who never used hedge phrases. His speech was full of flat, declaratory statements like, "That will never work" and "That's a dumb idea." He was universally disliked, mostly because of his insistence on using a communication style that never softened his negative statements. Using a hedge phrase would have made him seem more approachable and might have encouraged people to continue to come up with new ideas in the future. As women, we don't usually have to worry about using too few hedge phrases.

When you're speaking to men, or when you're in a hierarchically structured conversation, make a conscious effort to eliminate hedge phrases, because they can be seen as signs of insecurity and weakness.

2. Asking Too Many Questions

Asking questions is an excellent technique to get others to open up to us, and to draw them into the conversation. Like any other conversational element, it can be overused. "What did you think about the presentation?" can be used to include the other person and to essentially say, "I'd like to hear your opinion," or, "I don't want to force my opinion on you if you disagree." Be careful, though—we can get so used to asking questions that we begin to hide behind them. To men, asking constant questions can make us sound as if we have no opinion.

At work, the next time you're about to ask your usual questions, try a probing declaration instead, "John, bring me up to speed on the Acme project." Or, try the most useful probe of all, "Tell me about it."

3. It's Like, You Know?

Ending your statement on an upward inflection is a way of sneaking a question in even if the words themselves don't ask one—you do it with your tone of voice instead. "I would like a comparable salary increase(?)" The listener knows you don't really expect more money at all. You can sneak upward inflections into your statement in the middle also, "Monday won't work, I don't think(?), so Tuesday will be better." Even though your inflection went down at the end, it still signaled your indecision and hesitancy in the middle. Finally, watch out for one other way you can sound indecisive—simply fading away at the end of your statement, as if you lost steam, or forgot what you were saying.

A great technique to use is to end everything but the most direct question with a downward inflection. Even questions sound stronger with a downward inflection. "Would you agree?"

4. Tagging Questions onto Your Statements

- "That's a good idea, don't you think?"
- "You want me to follow through on this, right?"
- "It's getting hot in here, isn't it?"

In an all-female group the tag question, "It's getting hot in here, isn't it?" can be a genuine question. It essentially says, "I don't want to freeze everyone else out of the room if I'm the only one who's getting warm." Men hear tag questions, "The figures aren't working, are they?" as a request for reassurance or indecisiveness on your part.

5. Qualifying What You're about to Say

- "I sort of thought we could look over these projections . . ."
- "I have a little problem with this marketing plan."
- "I was just wondering if . . ."
- "I guess my question is . . ."

All these qualifiers share the same problem. They make it sound as if you discount your own words. The next time you start to qualify what you're about to say, ask yourself if the qualifier adds useful information. If it doesn't, leave it out.

6. ONE TEENY, WEENY MISTAKE: INTENSIFIERS

- "I was really excited to get the opportunity . . ."
- "I was so pleased when . . ."
- "It was a sensational presentation."

We use intensifiers when we intend to emphasize a point— "This isn't important, it is *really* important." Unfortunately, using intensifiers can signal that we don't expect to be listened to, so we have to intensify what we're saying to be heard at all. Who uses more intensifiers than anyone else? Children. They intensify what they are saying to get adults to pay attention: "Mom, this is really, really, really, really important." Ironically, eliminating intensifiers like "so," "just," "terribly," "really," and "very" can make you sound much stronger.

> It's the power to communicate your own positive human qualities, as well as information, that inspires people and energizes organizations.
>
> —*Joan Kenley, Ph.D.*

Be careful to eliminate intensifiers from your written communication also. Was it a "really good presentation" or a "concise and well documented presentation"? Notice how the adjectives "concise" and "well documented" add information to your statement in a way that "really" never does.

7. USING TOUCHY-FEELY WORDS

- "I feel as if she's the best candidate for the job."
- "I feel good about this investment."
- "I like your idea."

In my seminars, women have more difficulty changing this last method of speaking than any other. Perhaps because we pride ourselves on being in touch with our emotions, or because we want to make the workplace a more humane place, we fill our speech with vague, touchy-feely words. Verbs such as "feel," "like," "hope," and "want" are vague and emotional. When we use action verbs such as, "think," "decide," "analyze," "consider," "evaluate" instead, we not only sound stronger, we are forced to choose the precise verb that truly conveys our thoughts. Do you "like this idea" or have you "evaluated this idea"? Do you "feel as if she's the best candidate" or have you "considered and ranked the candidates"?

If you do nothing else, change your fuzzy, emotional, feel-good verbs to strong and accurate action verbs. You will not only sound stronger, you will begin to think with more clarity.

Strong, Not Tough

Notice that none of my suggestions makes you sound tough or aggressive. Coming across tough and aggressive broadcasts to the listener, "I expect you to disagree. I expect you to give me a hard time." Strength, on the other hand, can include warmth, compassion, friendship, even graciousness, while it still achieves results.

As we move to a more diverse work force and to a more participative management style, the strengths inherent in women's communication will be increasingly useful. Skills such as consensus building and attentiveness to nonverbal communication will always serve us well. Yet the seven typical female speech patterns I've discussed almost never serve us, whether we're talking with men or with other women. Eliminating these sabotaging speech patterns won't have you speaking or acting like a "tough" man. It will mean that you start using the language of success to sound like what you already are—a strong and successful woman.

ACTION STEPS
TO THE LANGUAGE OF SUCCESS

1. Become more aware of the two Gender Cultures and of the invisible rules that govern conversations. Notice, for example, if "turn-taking" or interruption is used, or whether banter and teasing are expected. Adapt your style to the group, even if it feels uncomfortable at first. Becoming more adept, more "bilingual," in our male–female communication can eliminate some of the seemingly senseless misunderstandings that damage our relationships.

2. Eliminate self-deprecatory remarks in front of men.

3. Be aware that men's teasing, razzing, put-down humor can signal inclusion in the group.

4. Turn your questions into statements. Avoid tag questions, and stop ending your statements on an upward inflection.

5. Stop hedging your bets. Ask yourself, "Does this phrase makes me sound more certain or less certain?" and stop discounting what you're about to say before you say it.

6. Eliminate qualifiers and intensifiers. If you want to emphasize a word, do it by stretching the word out slightly, and saying it with a lower pitch.

7. Make a list of strong, action verbs: decide, evaluate, consider, analyze, innovate, create. Use them, not only in your speech, but in your written communication as well.

About the Author

A communications specialist, **Julie White, Ph.D.,** has been a successful international speaker, seminar leader, consultant, and author for more than two decades. Her field of expertise includes both verbal and nonverbal communication, listening skills, presentation and briefing skills, and gender-related issues. In particular, her presentation on "The Gender Trap: New Insights on Communication Differences Between Men and Women" has been widely acclaimed as a humorous, nonthreatening, nonjudgmental approach to resolving misunderstandings and promoting a positive environment at work and at home. Julie's clients include Fortune 500 companies, sales organizations, health-care centers, governmental agencies, and international associations. She is the author of *Image and Self-Projection* and *Self-Esteem for Women*, two of the 10 all-time bestselling professional development training audiotapes.

Julie White, Ph.D.
President, Julie White & Associates
1101 Galloway Drive
El Paso, TX 79902
Phone: (800) 322-6033
Fax: (915) 533-3317
E-mail: *jwhitespkr@aol.com*
Web site: *www.JulieWhite.net*

chapter nine

Manage Your Time, Manage Your Life

Nanci McGraw
President, McGraw Communications

During my many years as a broadcaster, producing reports, features, and documentaries, I interviewed hundreds of people. For various news stories, I talked to actors, artists, authors, architects, business people at every level, taxi drivers, mechanics, bank tellers, doctors, ice skaters, models, lion tamers, Olympic champions, parents, photographers, zookeepers, and many more. It always intrigued me that some of them were able to distinguish themselves and move ahead of the pack in their chosen field.

In spite of events, people, or circumstances that could slow them down or stop them, why do some people still move ahead and not others? The difference, I believe, comes from whether or not they understand that how they manage their time is really about how they manage their lives.

Time management *is* life management. And managing our lives involves three actions: Choosing, Preparing, and Doing.

Choosing means looking this life over, holding a clear vision of what you want your life to look like, and making the choices necessary to bring that picture into focus. Florence Nightingale said, "Since I was twenty-four, there never was any vagueness in my plans or ideas as to what God's work was for me." Dr. Stephen Covey, author of *Seven Habits of Highly Effective People*, shared with me the power of single-mindedly selecting proper priorities in life. Choosing is the first step.

> Do not squander your time, for that is the stuff life is made of.
>
> —*Benjamin Franklin*

Preparing means defining, outlining, blueprinting, and planning. Abraham Lincoln said, "If I had eight hours to chop down a tree, I'd spend six hours sharpening the ax." Joan Embery, Goodwill Ambassador for the San Diego Zoo, spent years learning about animals in general, countless hours with the specific animals she would show on the *Tonight Show*, and then logged more than 75 appearances—all because of her preparation.

Doing means action. Follow-through. No excuses. Concert pianist Jan Paderewski once claimed, "Before I was a genius, I was a drudge." Candy Lightner, founder of M.A.D.D. (Mothers Against Drunk Drivers) told me that she literally parked herself at the office of the California governor and badgered them until her persistent presence and public speeches changed attitudes, laws, and penalties. Cookie entrepreneur Debbie Fields revealed that when she started her business no one came into the "Mrs. Fields Cookies" store, so she walked outside with a tray of cookies and gave them away.

> *The song I came to sing remains unsung. I have spent my life in stringing and unstringing my instrument.*
>
> —TAGORE RABINDRANATH

Many people choose and prepare, but then stop there. I call them the Watchers, the Dreamers, the Wishers, the Think-about-it-ers, or the Someday-I'll-ers. Other people distinguish themselves by their actions. Thus, I call them the DO-ers.

"Life Rewards the DO-ers!"

We have all met these people. DO-ers are successful people in any line of work. Denis Waitley, speaker and author of *Psychology of Winning*, asserts that "winners are willing to do what losers won't." That's the essence: the doing. Just knowing what to do is never enough.

When I present keynotes and seminars I ask the audience, "When was the last time you got paid for sitting in your chair at your desk and just 'knowing' how to do the job?" There is always a giggle and then a silence. No one gets paid for just 'knowing.' The paycheck comes because you tell, train, consult, type, design, dance, repair, climb, fix, propose, write, contact, sell, invent, inspire, plan—the action verbs are endless. Success lies in the verbs, not the nouns. Business guru, and author of *In Search of Excellence*, Tom Peters says that in order to be successful, we must "have a bias for action."

> My motto is "Add Zip to Your Trip!" and it feels "zo zippy" to get organized! It's almost a religious experience to plan and then accomplish.
>
> —*Nanci McGraw*

Never be impressed with what someone knows. Knowing is never enough. Only be impressed (if you're going to be impressed) with what they DO with what they know. And it's the same for each of us. Never be impressed with what you yourself know. We know a lot. We are smart people. Be impressed only by what you DO with what you know.

Taking Control of Your Time, Your Space, and Your Life

No mincing of words here: personal and professional organization is the key for DO-ers. This is not a tangential skill. Getting organized is

> No one gets paid for just "knowing." The paycheck comes . . . because of endless action verbs.
>
> —*Nanci McGraw*

the essence of being able to make things happen. DO-ers use this skill every day in many different ways: with their papers, desk, calendar, activities, priorities, and relationships.

When I have remembered to incorporate these skills into my own life, wonderful things have happened. I can look back and see how I achieved my desired results. When I've forgotten them or ignored them, nothing much happened. Those are the times that life felt stalled, and I felt confused and unhappy. Look into your own life, past and present. Check to see if the following skills are alive, well, and working for you. Remember, knowing them is not enough.

The DO-ers Top 10 Time/Life-Managing Skills

1. SET GOALS

We all have wishes, yearnings, or hankerings. However, until we commit to the B.E.S.T. kind of goals, nothing happens. B.E.S.T. goals are Believable, Energizing, Specific, and Time-bound. Write them down using this format. Writing creates an extra groove in the gray matter. That groove promotes commitment on our part. It helps move us to separate out the things we want to be doing from those things we don't want to waste any more time on. Equally as important as writing down what you DO want to do is writing down what you know you DON'T want to do.

2. BE FLEXIBLE

Ecclesiastes reminds us " . . . there is a time and season for every purpose under heaven . . ." I believe that. Some goals can be bumped ahead and sped up; others need to lie dormant until it is the right place and time for them. There is a time to prepare, and a time to move from preparation to tackling the goals themselves.

In 1979 I was happily married, with three wonderful children. When I looked around, I saw many women in broadcasting and felt a hunger inside to somehow include that in my life again. (As a teenager I had hosted a radio program.) My good husband encouraged me to feed that hunger. He prodded and encouraged until I wrote the goal down and ended up making an audition tape.

> Just knowing is never enough. We become what we do. Life rewards the DO-ers!
>
> —*Nanci McGraw*

When I mentioned my goal to my extended family, one relation commented, "Don't they want young people?" (Some people are ready to throw cold water on your hot dreams. Don't let them.) I spent the necessary preparing time. I created the checklists, sent out the tapes, made the phone calls, and then the callbacks. Finally someone took a chance on me. Less than 10 years later the news releases read, "News Director Nanci McGraw Wins 101st Broadcast Award." I started all that when I was thirty years old. Goals can be accomplished in the right "season."

3. PRIORITIZE

President Calvin Coolidge said, "We cannot do everything at once, but we can do something at once." Admitting that we cannot get everything done is a first step in managing our day, every day, and our lives. Often the best we can do is ask, "What is the best thing I could do right now?" Life is really a series of now points. It is interesting what things come to the front of the line, when we analyze them like that. All crises are not created equal.

4. SAY "YES" AND "NO"

Enthusiastically embrace those events, classes, tasks, and activities that provide the greatest support for your current goals. We often are involved in things that don't feed us, teach us, move us, inspire us anymore. And we stay involved because we have not admitted to ourselves that we've outgrown them.

It takes great self-control sometimes to divest ourselves gracefully of these involvements. We know what they are: anything that does not keep us focused on our goals, or that eats up precious time, which could be directed to tasks of greater personal value. People respect a focused, helpful, not overly committed contributor. Better to do a great job at a few things, than an off-and-on job at many.

5. DELEGATE

... and tolerate. This one is for those who have a tendency to be distracted by details. Stifle the urge to clean up every mess. Let it go. Get others involved and be glad for any help, even though the job they do may not be quite up to your expectations. Sometimes the better choice is to raise the tolerance for slight disarray, because not to do so makes us slaves to what I call the "fuss and foofoo" syndrome. We take time to fidget, fix, and fuss with something, even when we would be better off to put our efforts elsewhere.

6. SELECT

Once, a local television station wanted to interview me and produce a feature on the topic of getting organized. I suggested that they let a cameraperson follow me as I peeked into all the anchors' offices. I moved into one newsman's office and found his desk and walls to be virtually covered with museum-like memorabilia, with very little place to work. I used mock seriousness to make one of my signature points, "What we have here is a high Doodad Ratio."

> Getting organized is the essence of being able to make things happen.
>
> —Nanci McGraw

Here are two important tips. First, pick material possessions that require less care and keeping. Choose carefully the fabrics, surfaces, equipment, and objects that you let into your life. Maintaining our possessions can take time, eat energy, stifle creativity, and slow down productivity. Second, beware of things that just sit there and do nothing. They are treacherous for life management. Control "stuff" acquisition by choosing carefully. "Down with Doodads!"

7. ANALYZE

There is a time for being efficient and a time, as Dr. Stephen Covey says, to slow down in order to be more effective. Life often goes from crisis to crisis. Many times a crisis could have been avoided if only we had taken the time at some point to analyze, "What would I do if . . . ?" The important concept is to sometimes slow down in order to speed up.

> Life is really a series of now points. It is interesting what things come to the front of the line, when we analyze it like that. All crises are not created equal.
>
> —*Nanci McGraw*

In my seminars I teach how to stop, look, listen, and really scrutinize the process, the path, the work, the systems. Be willing to admit that if you can't find something or do something without a lot of trouble, it's because (A) you don't have a system; (B) you aren't using your system; (C) you need a new system. This reality therapy always draws laughs for its absolute in-your-face honesty. I have proved to myself every time I have trouble, that the answer lies here. If A or B is true, then implement C!

8. CHOOSE

Deliberately do things differently. Be a contrarian. This means forming the habit of doing things directly the opposite of how the rest of the world would do it. Shop earlier in the morning or later at night. Go to the bank during non-payday weeks and times. When others are commuting, you choose to time shift. When others take holidays, you choose to work. Celebrate winter holidays after the calendar says so, to take advantage of the sales. Contrarians make it a practice of finding the unworn path. Taking that path can save time, money, effort, energy, pain, and relationships.

A professional colleague told me she makes an effort to live by the contrarian code and can speak of untold benefits. It takes focus and commitment, though, and willingness to be different.

9. MAXIMIZE

Everyone has his or her own rhythm. Being true to your rhythm means being in touch with your body and how you work. It means watching how you react when you eat certain foods. It means discovering your prime times when you are most focused, alert, creative, and clear-headed. It means discovering your downtimes when you are tired, listless, less energetic, and easily confused or distracted.

> Discover your Prime Times . . . and admit your Downtimes. Maximize both.
>
> —*Nanci McGraw*

As you plan your day, you can maximize both your prime times and downtimes, by matching your tasks to the most effective mental and physical state for carrying them out. For example, assign your acute mental work to your morning prime time when you're sharp, and return phone calls to the midafternoon downtime when conversation would be welcome.

I have seminar participants who commit to planning their up and downtimes, and being ready to change their mood, with music, laughter, a brisk walk, a glass of water, or a fun toy at their desk. Those who follow through, and turn this proactive planning into doing, report real success in their life management.

10. LEARN WHEN TO BE PERFECT

Perfectionism can be the sign of a true professional. It can also be a time waster. Sometimes it matters to achieve perfection, but often it really doesn't. Distinguish between those times. There's an old adage I've found useful: "Often done is good enough."

In my book *Organized for Success!* I offer some insightful questions for us to ask ourselves whenever we feel the urge to keep working too long on something, to keep fiddling with it:

- Will the results be substantially better if I put in more effort?
- Will I get paid more?
- Would anyone else notice the improvements?
- Would anyone else even care?
- Have I gone as far as I can without getting help?
- Have I already done more than is expected of me?

DO-ers know when to keep working on a task. DO-ers also know when to quit, when that task gets to the point of diminishing returns.

British statesman and former prime minister Benjamin Disraeli said, "As a general rule, the most successful people in life are those who have the best information." For people who end up with something to show for their dreams, I believe it means even going one better than that. It means using the information in ways that work best to create the success. It means managing life by managing time—by putting this information to work. Just knowing is never enough. All the DO-ers I've ever interviewed, observed, or read about know the drill: life means choosing, then planning, and finally doing. There is no other way.

TOP 10 LIFE MANAGEMENT SKILLS FOR DO-ERS

1. **Set goals.** Wishes get you nowhere, except in fairy tales.
2. **Be flexible.** There is a time and season for many goals.
3. **Prioritize.** All crises are not created equal.
4. **Say "Yes."** Focus on the people, activities, and tasks that move your goals ahead.
5. **Delegate and tolerate.** Learn to put up with less than the antiseptic, orderly, and finished.
6. **Select.** Pick carefully those things that require care and keeping.

7. **Analyze.** Efficiency saves time and money; slow down to speed up.
8. **Choose.** Select off hours and times: the contrarian lifestyle can free up extra hours.
9. **Maximize.** Discover your prime times and downtimes and use both to advantage.
10. **Learn when to be perfect.** Use perfectionism to advantage, so it's not a waste of time.

Or Look at the Flip Side.

THESE 10 "NEGATIVES" CAN YIELD POSITIVELY INCREDIBLE SUCCESS

1. **Be stubborn.** Select a goal and go for it. Don't let people discourage you.
2. **Be resigned.** Acknowledge and take joy in the natural flow of life, changes, and seasons.
3. **Procrastinate.** Avoid the low priorities, so the important things can rise to the top.
4. **Be negative.** Learn how to say "no," so you can focus on what will bring positive results.
5. **Be messy.** Increase your tolerance for a little disarray. This will free up some time.
6. **Be fussy.** Be careful about acquiring more "stuff" in your life and physical environment.
7. **Go slowly.** See the process clearly and create a system, which will allow you thereafter to go faster.
8. **Be contrary.** Do things when other people don't, in order to avoid crowds and save time.
9. **Be lazy.** Discover the rhythm of your body and your life to maximize your productivity.
10. **Be mediocre.** Learn what needs to be done well and reserve the perfectionism for those things only.

About the Author

Nanci McGraw, president of McGraw Communications, has been described as a "passionate communicator with creative, clear ideas." She presents up to 150 programs annually across the United States and in Canada and Asia. Topics include "Life Rewards the DO-ers!"; "Get Organized"; "Ready, Set, GOAL!"; and "Communicate for Success!" Nanci sparkles with the creativity that won her more than 100 broadcasting awards, including two "Golden Mikes," six AP "Mark Twains," and reports on ABC, NBC, and Associated Press. Her happy clients include Avis, Boeing, Eli Lilly, Hewlett-Packard, IBM, Marriott, Motorola, and VISA. Nanci is the author of two books: *Organized for Success!* and *Speak Up and Stand Out!* She has an Internet radio program, "Life Rewards the DO-ers!" and an online newsletter, "I Can DO That!"

Nanci McGraw, President
McGraw Communications
P.O. Box 178424
San Diego, CA 92177-8424
Phone: (800) 578-2278, (858) 279-9496 (San Diego, CA)
E-mail: *nanci@nanci.org*
Web site: *www.nanci.org*

chapter ten

The Seven Stepping Stones to Success

PEGGY EDDY, CFP

President, Creative Capital Management, Inc.

As I reflect upon my life, I see seven themes that have been constants and the stepping stones to my success. They are (1) having a purpose for being; (2) relying on my intuition when taking risks; (3) being persistent; (4) making use of my particular talents; (5) maintaining a clear vision of the outcomes I desire; (6) having my own business; and (7) creating a balance, albeit a delicate one, between my family, business, and spiritual life.

Having a Purpose in Life

I've never sought success in order to get fame and money; it's the talent and the passion that counts in success.

—INGRID BERGMAN

If you were to interview the most successful individuals alive today, perhaps the most singular common response to why they are such successes would be that they followed their passion. To be truly successful, I believe you must have a life's purpose that propels you into the future and creates contentment.

I have always believed that if we only go this way once, *doing what we truly love doing is the foundation of success*. In my business, having the opportunity to positively affect my clients' financial lives and help them fulfill lifelong dreams is thrilling. True, the detail work with financial data is not the most exciting component of my work. However, the end results are exciting: The widow who tells me that, under my tutelage, she has taken control of her household finances for the first time. The entrepreneur who grows her business under my professional guidance and sells it to a public company. Helping clients achieve greater financial peace of mind is what gets me up in the mornings, embracing the challenges that the day will bring.

Taking Calculated Risks and Using Intuition Well

And the trouble is, if you don't risk anything, you risk even more.

—ERICA JONG

The interviewer was talking to the young Marine officer who was applying for the career placement services her firm provided. There was a calmness and self-assuredness about him that was appealing. Confident that he could do well in his job interviews, she assigned him a time to meet with the recruiter for an engineering firm and he jokingly assured her he wouldn't embarrass her. Following his interview, he called to report the results and took her off guard when he asked her out for dinner. She had made it a practice never to socialize with job applicants. But this time, relying on her intuition, she accepted the date. She has been enjoying his company for almost 27 years as his wife, business partner, and mother of their two sons.

> The purpose of life is a life of purpose.
>
> —*Robert Byrne*

I tell this story because it was unlike me to go outside the safe harbor of rules I had set for myself. If I had not listened to my "inner voice"—intuition, gut reaction, visceral indicator—I would not have gone out on that date and would have missed marrying the love of my life, my husband and business partner, Bob. Taking that chance and doing something spontaneously led to an exciting, vibrant life of owning our own business and raising two fine sons together.

When Succeeding Is the Only Choice, Persistence Is the Key

Four months after we were married we chose to start a business in San Diego. As we were both highly employable, we felt we could always get "real jobs" if the business didn't grow. We decided that with no children, no mortgage, and a negative net worth, we had little to lose. *There was no choice but to succeed.*

For our first three months in business, we went door to door calling on small business owners. Finally, one magical day, with less than $300 left in our personal checking account, Bob signed up our first client. We were on our way!

As they say, persistence pays off. Continuing to work your plan, even in the face of failure, eventually results in success, regardless of the financial outcome. The strength of character you build from persisting in the face of challenging situations lasts far longer than the impact of getting that one client.

Lead from Your Strengths: Hire Out What You Cannot Do

> *There are two kinds of talent, man-made talent and God-given talent. With man-made talent you have to work very hard. With God-given talent, you just touch it up once in a while.*
>
> —PEARL BAILEY

In my opinion, our business has flourished for 25 years because my husband and I have complementary talents that blend harmoniously. I think of us as "co-preneurs." During the early years of the business, although I could do tax returns and balance sheets, placing numbers on the correct lines was not fulfilling or creative enough work for me. So I decided to focus on what I enjoyed most—writing, interpreting tax laws for clients, educating clients about their money and investment portfolios, putting together informational evening programs for women clients, speaking on financial topics for organizations, and meeting with clients on a regular basis to evaluate their financial progress.

As we breathed life into our business, we clearly delineated our individual responsibilities based on our respective skills and preferences. This blending of our abilities has enabled our enterprise to provide our clients with the best possible service.

I believe that creating a confluence of God-given talent with brainpower contributes greatly to a business's success. I also believe that a successful businessperson needs to "hire out" those tasks for which they are ill-suited and build a good support team to supplement their expertise. For example, we routinely urge our entrepreneurial clients to establish advisory councils or active boards of directors to support their own talent in their respective businesses, creating their own personal think tank. Focusing on what you do best is a great stepping stone to success!

Be Your Own "CVO" (Chief Visionary Officer) and Convey Your Vision to Others

> *Dreams and wishes belong together. Dreams and wishes can be manifested.*
>
> —VIRGINIA SATIR

Without a vision or an idea of how you want your life to be and what you wish to accomplish in your family, community, career, or business, life is like so much "Jell-O on the wall." Having clearly defined goals is absolutely a necessity in order to succeed at anything. Using what I call the "SMART" system of goal setting works! Goals should be *specific, measurable, achievable, realistic, and time-bound.*

The first step is to envision your desired outcome. This needs to be a life mission statement, such as "becoming the first woman president of the company." To accomplish this mission, the steps to take must be written down with various "accomplishment dates." Note the words "written down." Committing goals to writing is imperative.

> You can forge a satisfying career by working hard at developing your natural talents into profitable skills.
>
> —*Dr. William Knaus*

In my financial planning practice, I spend a great deal of time with each client to determine his/her true financial priorities. Using financial data as keys to unlock the door to financial independence, the financial plan itself spells out clearly defined objectives, offering

> Clearly define the long-range goals you aspire to and all the obstacles in your way will become hills instead of mountains.
>
> —*O. A. Battista*

written recommendations and solutions for each area of financial concern. At the back of the planning document, I summarize the client's "financial homework" on a written implementation schedule. On that single sheet appear quantifiable goals and targeted completion dates. Clients have told me that the one-page "map" has provided them with a clear direction and time frame within which to reach their financial milestones. The clients who follow the written goal sheet experience tremendous feelings of success and achieve financial peace of mind as they work their plan.

Remember that the SMART system used the words "realistic" and "achievable" in the goal-setting exercise. Honestly assessing your skills, your financial status, your family situation, and your work life can result in a meaningful, thorough life vision.

Having a mental picture of the outcome you wish to create is also helpful. When allowed to dream and envision the successful completion of well defined goals, the mind can be an incredible ally. "Think it and you will achieve it" is an excellent mantra to practice at points in your life when success may seem elusive.

Owning a Business Provides True Personal and Financial Freedom

> *The woman who can create her own job is the woman who will win fame and fortune.*
>
> —AMELIA EARHART

To provide a woman with the greatest amount of flexibility, creativity, self-reliance, success, and control in her life, being self-employed is the best opportunity in America today. Owning one's own business can provide the financial freedom to educate our children, fund our retirement, and help support our aging parents. And the outlook for women-owned businesses is bright: they make up the fastest growing segment of our economy.

Work and home life can be blended by operating a home-based business and utilizing technology to leverage time and earnings potential. The "virtual office" has created the opportunity for a woman to be online with a client while supervising a child's homework project from her home office.

Having a service business has provided me with an arena in which my nurturing skills are valued and can produce profits. Caring for clients in a highly personalized manner has paid large dividends, which are reflected in the business's bottom line. In the face of competition, particularly in the financial services area today, this "hi tech–high touch" approach has worked consistently well.

Survival Skills for the Self-Employed Woman

What survival skills are helpful to develop as a self-employed woman? First, use the SMART goal-setting system and develop a written business plan. I hold a business planning meeting off-site with Bob and our staff each year. We review the plan from last year, evaluate our progress on the written implementation schedule, and establish meaningful goals for the next 12 months. Each month we review where we are on the time-bound list of achievements and redirect our efforts to stay "on task." Having well developed business systems and financial statements that correctly reflect the financial status of a business are crucial to a businesswoman's success.

Next, hire only the absolute best help you can find. Most of my frustration as a business owner comes from the fact that employees will never treat my business with the care and attention that I do. Hiring staff with a strong work ethic is my main goal.

Third, do not work with clients or customers who make you sick or angry. Annually, we make a list of clients who no longer fit into our major areas of service. Generally, these are the clients who are the most demanding and less than polite to us and our staff.

> Striving for excellence
> motivates you; striving
> for perfection is
> demoralizing.
>
> —*Harriet Braiker*

These clients receive a very nice letter from me, which gently summarizes the various areas of service that have not completely delighted them. The letter ends by suggesting that another firm could serve them better.

Fourth, take time off. When I find I am spending too much time at the office and do not control my own calendar to allow myself time off, I become resentful and less productive. Some of my best creative ideas come during the time I am working in my rose garden or walking in the quiet of the morning. Allowing yourself time to dream and reflect is crucial to remaining focused and energized in your business.

Fifth, acknowledge your mistakes and apologize to clients when you make errors. No one is perfect. Remember, "excellence, not perfection." As much as we women hate to admit it, we do not always know the answer or always do the perfect thing. I have found, in instances where I have erred or disappointed a client, that contacting the client to point out the mistake, offering to rectify it, and conveying my apology is better than trying to avoid the situation. As difficult as it is to acknowledge that I, too, am human, most of my clients appreciate my forthright approach and quickly absolve me of any guilt.

Sixth and last, cut your losses. If you hire the wrong person, lose money on a new product, misread the market, or buy a less than profitable subsidiary, as soon as you recognize the mistake, fix it! Do whatever it takes to stop the behavior, replace the staff person, or control the cash flow hemorrhage. Being self-employed is not for the weak-kneed.

Balancing Long-Term Investments of Time, Energy, and Commitment

All my possessions for a moment of time.

—ELIZABETH I, QUEEN OF ENGLAND

Bob and I were committed to raising our children ourselves. When the boys were infants and toddlers, we shared time caring for them and working in the business. Although it was not in vogue at the time, Bob was very present in their lives and "covered" for me when I needed to meet with clients during my two days out in the field.

When they started school, one of us was always present when Sean and Ryan left for elementary and high school and one of us was there in the afternoon to pick them up or to greet them after school. Owning the business provided us the opportunity to take off time for track meets and field trips, or to stay home when one of the boys was ill. In addition, despite the challenge it was to balance home life and the business demands, the message it sent to our children was that they were more important than the business.

Apparently, it was a very strong message. Recently, our younger son took us to dinner and told us, "I am as successful as I am so far because of your good parenting and always being there for me." Earlier this year, in an award-winning college essay, our older son wrote this: "While I realize the opportunities in business are endless, I know beyond a doubt that my parents have instilled in me those qualities—namely, integrity, initiative, independence, self-discipline, drive, and leadership—that will allow me to be flexible, as I actively follow my goal of starting a successful enterprise and *providing the love, support and opportunities for a family as my parents provided me*" (italics added).

Forfeiting financial gain in order to be present in my children's lives has resulted in the tremendous joy I feel knowing that I parented well. Being a successful mother while owning a business is achievable, once you determine what is most important in your life.

> Balancing a job and family is not the hardest thing to achieve. It's second. (Right after world peace.)
>
> **—Barbara and Jim Dale**

Final Remarks

Without question, these "Seven Stepping Stones to Success" have guided me well. They have taught me valuable lessons and helped me make informed choices, large and small, that I have made in my life. Having a satisfying and financially successful business, being fully human, accepting my limitations, greeting each day with joy, having a passion for what I do, having a strong faith, and basking in the love of my family are all blessings made possible because I applied myself to walk the balanced path marked by those stepping stones. May you be as well served by them as have I!

THE 7 STEPPING STONES
TO SUCCESS

1. Have a purpose in life.
2. Take calculated risks as part of achieving success in our world, and use your intuition.
3. Plan to succeed and be persistent.
4. Lead from your strengths and "hire out" what you cannot do.
5. Be your own CVO, "Chief Visionary Officer," and share your clear vision with others.
6. Own a business to achieve personal and financial freedom.
7. Become a success with long-term endeavors and commitment, but *have balance in your life.*

About the Author

Peggy Eddy, a Certified Financial Planner, is president of San Diego–based Creative Capital Management, Inc., founded by Peggy and her husband, Bob, in 1975. The author of a biweekly column on business and wealth management, she is a popular speaker at conferences on business and financial topics and a frequent guest on local and national radio and television programs.

Peggy has served as president and board member of the San Diego Chapter of Women in Business and public relations chair of the San Diego Society of the Institute of Certified Financial Planners, in addition to serving on numerous community boards, which include the boards of local chambers of commerce, the SBA Advisory Council for Region IX, and the Advisory Board of the San Diego Chamber of Commerce Small Business Development Center. Founding president of the San Diego Chapter of the National Association of Women Business Owners, Peg also founded the Family Business Institute at the University of San Diego in 1992 to encourage the continuity of family businesses.

Peggy Eddy, CFP
Creative Capital Management, Inc.
2650 Camino del Rio North, Suite 302
San Diego, CA 92108
Phone: (619) 298-3993
E-mail: *peg@creativecapitalmgt.com*

chapter eleven

Finding the Fear: Marketing 101

JACQUELINE TOWNSEND KONSTANTUROS
President and Chief Executive Officer, The Townsend Agency

If you never take a chance, you will never fail. If you have never failed, you were never taking a chance. Ask yourself, "Do I actualize my potential? Do I have the *fear*?"

Does your business have the fear? If you approach your business and the marketplace with critical mass and velocity, you should always be a little afraid. Just a slight tinge of fear should taint every interoffice memorandum, work plan, product schedule, and most importantly, your marketing campaign. Find the fear.

I started my full-service advertising agency more than seven years ago in a hole-in-the-wall office space with one employee and cardboard boxes for desks. We were afraid. Afraid that our children would never have the benefits that life has to offer. Afraid that debt would consume us and our business and drag our families underwater. Most of all, we were afraid of not becoming who we wanted to be. We struggled at first. But motivated each day by the fear nipping at our heels, we wanted to succeed. We chose to believe in ourselves. We wanted to beat the fear.

> If the USP (unique selling proposition) that your company offers solves a problem and delivers a benefit, shout it to the world!

In the business of public relations, marketing, and advertising, I meet with dozens of people every day who could use our services in some capacity or another. Every business needs a marketing communications plan. A plan that spells out who your company is, what it does, and where it is going. However, nobody wants to spend money on the intangibles. Spending is for product improvements and new technology. Spending isn't for marketing and advertising. Only the big companies need marketing, right?

Wrong. Everyone offers excuses for a lack of sufficient marketing. The biggest excuse for the absence of a marketing plan? It's too expensive. But wait, how much will it actually take for reasonable results? You'll be surprised. And if your company is serious, you'll be glad you spent it! The first comment I make to clients who say they need a marketing plan with big results is . . . *be afraid*. Be *very* afraid.

One question should permeate every piece of your company's marketing communications . . . *What keeps my customers up at night?* Now, how can my business solve that problem? Think strategically and act succinctly, that's how. Build a problem-solving business model through proper positioning, cohesive branding, and in-your-face marketing communications.

Building a Critical Stance

Positioning. What exactly does that mean? Don't sit too close to the television set? Keep your arms and legs inside the vehicle at all times? Not quite.

Positioning is your company's placement within the marketplace of similar products or services. Don't panic. Positioning doesn't just happen. It is best approached as a multi-tiered process consisting of strategic planning and market segmentation analysis. To make this easier to understand, I have prepared the following example to represent a consumer-based product. The same basic steps we look at here will apply to the business-to-business and direct-to-consumer segments as well.

Strategy begins with your current position within the market. Chances are that if you need positioning help, you're a little shaky on where your company stands now. So, assuming that you are striving to be number one in the market, let's begin with some positioning indicators. First, to figure out if your company has a positioning problem, take the following litmus test for poor positioning. Do internal groups become opposing camps instead of a synergistic team? Does the company appear reactive to market forces rather than proactive? Do you tend to follow the competition versus lead the pack? A "Yes" to any one of these questions indicates a potentially crippling stance within the market.

> Competition is the single largest threat to a company's survival. It's also the biggest opportunity in modern business.

Don't sell the farm and hock the hardware yet, though. Not everyone can be the market leader. The consumer body, as a whole, needs substitutes that compete based on price and quality. If not for this fact, Wal-Mart would never have left the ground! In laymens' terms, a company's actual ranking doesn't matter as much as market awareness. Let the consumer know that you "own" a position—as the leader, the quality substitute, or even the generic equivalent—in the market. All of these positions are valuable and can be leveraged with the correct marketing approach.

The path to developing a strong strategic position begins with knowing your customers and prospects. What do they sell? Where are they located? What do they look like? How do they react? This is your target market, the segment of the marketplace universe that could benefit in some way from what your company has to offer.

Next, determine your company's key prospects. List your top five desired clients. Then, decide what each prospect has in common with the others. Is it the buying structure? Are they similar in size or mobility? What is the collective thread that sews them together? The more you know about how your prospective customers relate to each other, the easier it becomes to tailor an efficient and effective marketing campaign to target their specific needs.

Don't be generic. Stand for something.

Once you have targeted your prospects, it's time to hone in on your differences from the competition. Why do your customers buy from you, as opposed to your competitors? This step will help your company decipher the unique product or selling aspect that separates your firm from the competition. This will reveal your most valuable trait in the marketplace . . . your *USP*, or *unique selling proposition*. The USP is the one thing at which your company excels, where others might be weak. It should be intimately woven into every marketing message your company gives/makes to prospective clients, who base their decisions on solutions and benefits. If the USP that your company offers solves a problem and delivers a benefit, shout it to the world!

At this point you should be feeling better about your company's placement out there among the myriad providers and vendors. The next step is to zoom in on the environment where your firm competes. Your market. To better understand the market and how it evolves, ask of your company, "How do the prospects that don't deal with us solve their problem? Is there an alternative resource? Are there substitutes in the marketplace? Is your product a luxury item or a necessity?"

Find the core consumers and talk directly to them.

Answering these questions honestly and in depth will shed some precious light on the marketplace and its competing forces. Do not offer stereotypes as solutions. Instead, determine what really makes the market react. What really makes the competition tick?

Once you know this, you can move to the next phase of designing a strategic position. Competition is the single largest threat to a company's survival. It's also the biggest opportunity in modern business. One major mistake that many small businesses make is attacking the competition at the wrong end. How many times have you heard, "Their strength is the running game, so we're going to stop the run"? Good positive outlook, bad strategic maneuver! What if the high-technology sector took that approach? Everyone would try to outdo Microsoft in the platform arena. Bad decision.

> When your company gets comfortable with its position and brand is precisely when you need to stay on your toes.

Hit them where they are weakest. How? Define your competition. List and name their greatest strengths. Be very aware of the existence of these powers and do not avoid them, but don't concentrate on them. Now, list and name your competition's primary weaknesses. This is where you focus your energy. If you have developed a good product and have positioned yourself correctly in the market, their weakness should be your strength.

The final phase of developing and constructing a dominant position is combining effective public relations, intelligent collateral materials, and thought-provoking advertising messages. Then, hit 'em. Hard.

Fearless Branding

Let's talk about you for a second. Do you want people to think highly of you? Are you considered among your friends to be valuable and loyal? Are your actions consistent with your words and thoughts? Can you adapt to new and changing environments without compromising who you are? If you can say yes to these questions, you have successfully branded yourself. Maybe you didn't realize it, but you are a *brand*. A singular person uniquely different from the masses of other human beings, and it is important not to lose that identity—your *brand identity*. Bring the fear into the branding strategy.

Branding in today's fickle, skeptical, and overcrowded marketplace is more valuable, in most instances, than the item or items being branded. Companies spend hundreds of millions of dollars every year ensuring that their products and services remain unique. And that you will buy into that uniqueness. We have gone so far as to create legal bolsters to guarantee these points of differentiation. We, as consumers, spend billions annually to adorn ourselves with the products that we associate with most clearly. We are reinforcing our own brand by buying into the brand identity of surrounding products and services.

Still a little confused? Have you ever said, "There is no way you would ever get me into that place"? Or how about, "I wouldn't be caught dead wearing that outfit"? Those statements reinforce who you are and, just as importantly, who you aren't.

Your business needs to approach branding in a similar manner. Don't be afraid to shun portions of the marketplace. You don't want to be the company or brand that tries to be all things to all people. It makes your brand fuzzy. Your company has to stand for something. Building an image is the most painstakingly arduous task that your business will ever endure.

It is monumentally important to do it right the first time. Because, as hard as it is to build a brand image, it is infinitely more difficult to reverse a poor image. Here are the key steps to ensure a sound, enduring, and comprehensive branding strategy.

First step: Don't be generic. Stand for something. Make the segment of the marketplace that you are focusing on passionate about your product. Breed loyalty. Seek conversion. Incite the fear. "How?" you ask. Here's the answer using an example. How many of your friends are Coca-Cola drinkers and simply will not drink a Pepsi? You might be one! Similarly, if they're Pepsi drinkers and the distributor has only Coca-Cola, then it's time to order something else. The customers of either one will swear up-and-down that the taste of the other is too sweet, too strong, or too something. Why? Because it's not their brand. That is fear.

> Realize that the market is a fragile environment and that it necessitates constant adaptation. Stay on the edge.

Next step: Find the core consumers and talk directly to them. If the core consumers are technology savvy, upper-middle-income thirty-somethings, talk to them **where they play**. If you bombard the core consumer only at their place of work, chances are you're missing their attention; they've got their advertising guard up. Instead, build a friendship. Don't just rely on the *Wall Street Journal* or *Information Week*. Go to their leisure time activities and spend some quality time building a relationship. Show up in *Wired Magazine*. Peek out of *GQ*. Sponsor a local gala event. To truly be heard by the core consumer, you need to reach them when they have their guard down. Frighten them. Make them ask "What are *they* doing here?" Once they've noticed your business, give them some information they can use. Tell them that you have a brand that fits their lifestyle. Then treat them like you care about their business. Because if you don't, someone else will!

> Shake up the competition. Then, shake up your core consumer.

Caveat: Comfort Zone

You've positioned your firm successfully. Your branding strategy is working on multiple levels. Your company is reaping the benefits of effective marketing tactics. Time to sit back and work on that golf handicap, right? Buzz! Wrong answer. Judges, tell them what they've lost . . . *the competitive edge*.

So many companies find this out too late. When your company gets comfortable with its position and brand is precisely when you need to stay on your toes. Younger, smaller companies generally have more flexibility and can quietly sneak up on your customers.

Protect your equity in the marketplace by continually re-evaluating your image and target audience. Are you losing your core customer because of lack of service? Is the competition stealing market share? Using the litmus test you designed earlier, regularly ask if your business is sitting back and becoming a victim of someone else's more effective or efficient marketing techniques.

Heighten the fear. Realize that the market is a fragile environment and that it necessitates constant adaptation. Consumer focus and interest is saturated by invasive, intuitive, and intrusive marketing efforts. Stay on the edge. Insist that your company stay on the forefront of technology. Invest in the image that you have built. The market has become accustomed to your business leading the field. Don't disappoint them. Be afraid. Afraid that your position is in jeopardy. Use the fear to your advantage.

How? Shake up the competition. This is effectively achieved by pervasive public relations. Have your PR firm release company-specific and market segment–specific information. For example, let the competition know that you've hired on an exceptional new talent in the industry. Send out reports on the market trends, followed closely with your firm's current successes in leading these trends. Keep your competition on the trailing end of an uphill battle.

> There is nothing more liberating or relaxing than bright, vivid success.

Then, shake up your core consumers. Make them aware of flaws in any current technologies or methods. Offer them solutions to these challenges. If the market landscape is turning in a new direction, change your marketing strategy. Never think that even the most loyal customer won't leave. If they start to think that you're lagging behind the learning curve, they will . . . they'll leave in hordes, like lemmings leaping off a cliff!

Remember that *the Comfort Zone* is not where you are invited to reflect on past successes. It's where you plan for the future and sharpen your company's stance within the marketplace. It's also a time of volatility. Realize that the competition is waiting in the shadows for this opportunity to come to fruition. Use your standing in the marketplace to reinforce your own company image. Emphasize your strengths with benefits to the consumer. Also, pour resources and energy into your weaknesses—the competition is focusing on them. Use the fear to be aware of the seams in your armor. Your company's greatest asset can be the ability to recognize and fortify its own flaws.

Lastly, after your company has secured a leading position, built a strong brand, and increased its adaptability quotient, stay focused! Find the fear. There is nothing more liberating or relaxing than bright, vivid success. Enjoy it.

10 STEPS TO FEARLESS SUCCESS

1. Motivate from within and radiate positive energy. The only thing that will ever stop you from obtaining everything you want out of life is your own laziness.
2. Decide to succeed. It is your choice, make it a clear one.
3. Be passionate—about your company, about yourself, and about every second you're alive.
4. Remember your customer's needs and fulfill them with zeal.
5. Think strategically, and you will always have a road map to your location.
6. Hire only the best and brightest people—then get out of their way!
7. Compete with honesty and ferocity. The marketplace will love you for it.
8. Remain infinitely adaptable. Never allow yourself or your company to settle for *good enough*.
9. Find the fear in everything that you do. Let it invigorate your senses instead of dominate them.
10. Insist on being bigger than you are. Don't make a splash . . . create a tidal wave! Go big. Go loudly. And go all out.

About the Author

As president and CEO of the Townsend Agency, **Jacqueline Townsend Konstanturos** combines a powerful mix of in-depth knowledge with years of strategic marketing, planning, and implementation. She earned her masters degree in science, graduating summa cum laude from Wright State University. She travels across the country several times a year on press tours, representing clients to trade and national business publications with results that are unparalleled in the marketing industry. She is also a much sought-after speaker at industry events and has made presentations to groups such as MIT Forum, High Tech Direct 2000, and the International Society of Technical Communicators.

Jacqueline Townsend Konstanturos
President and CEO
The Townsend Agency
10180 Telesis Court, 5th Floor
San Diego, CA 92121
Phone: (858) 457-4888 x136
Fax: (858) 453-7010
E-mail: *jtk@townsendagency.com*
Web site: *www.townsendagency.com*

chapter twelve

Taming Technology

JEANETTE S. CATES, PH.D.
CEO, TechTamers

Have you noticed that things are moving faster? Do you feel like you're being swallowed by the undergrowth in the jungle of technology and may never get out? Are you afraid that technology will take control of your life? You're not alone.

As a little girl I played in my grandparents' home office. My favorite machines were the typewriter and the adding machine—the one with 10 keys and a crank on the side. I could control those. I understood how they worked and I could get them to do what I asked—even at the age of three! But I was afraid of the big mechanical calculator. It was huge. It had 10 rows of buttons and was at least a dozen columns wide. When you punched in numbers and asked the calculator to do something, its moving head nodded and shook until the answer came out. Once, I tried to "test" it and gave it so many numbers to calculate it went wild. It kept calculating and calculating and calculating. I swear it was smoking! I finally unplugged it and left the room quickly. I don't know that I ever asked it to do something again.

Fast forward 20 years. I was in college. The campus was all abuzz with the news of the new "computer." A Sunday Open House was held so that all of us "regular people" (read nonengineers) could see it. We filed past a glass window in the engineering building, paying homage to a large box with blinking links and whirring tapes. One of the engineering students was playing chess with it and I wondered why? Because it just reminded me of that big old calculator on Granddaddy's desk—the one I never wanted to play with again.

In the early 1980s, two incidents coincided for me. First, I went back to graduate school to earn my masters in adult education. Second, to support my education habit, I got a temporary job in the State Comptroller's Office doing data entry. On the first day, our supervisor took us on a tour of the mainframe. It was behind a glass wall and it was huge! All of my old fears began to surface.

Our first assignment was to get acquainted with the data entry terminals. My station was in a long room, about 50 feet from that glass wall. I faced it and was very conscious of the mainframe watching me. Near the end of the morning, our supervisor did a strange thing. She said, "I want you to try to break the mainframe. Do whatever you like at your workstation, but try to make smoke come out." Now I had had experience with that smoke thing and I felt certain I could replicate it. I began to put in more numbers than I could count. I typed faster. I laid my arm on the keyboard and rolled it back and forth, all the time watching the mainframe behind its glass wall. Suddenly, it began to smile at me. I could hear it saying, "You can't hurt me. I will work for you no matter what you do." That mainframe and I had a three-month relationship— and I never was able to make smoke pour out of its ears!

During the last 20 years that I have consulted with companies to help them use technology more effectively, I've heard some of the same concerns repeatedly:

"It's out of control!"

"We don't know where to begin."

"A lot of our computers are sitting idle."

"We're not getting a good return on our investment of time and money!"

To help my clients deal with these dilemmas, I have identified eight major areas that make the difference between taming technology and its getting the better of you. We'll look at each of these to see how they can affect you and your company.

The first thing we need to do is to fight back the encroaching jungle. We need to get a sense of control. Here's where the 4 Ts— technology, training, time, and team support—provide our first line of defense.

Technology Is the Start

You must start with the technology itself. What do you have? How current is it? Is it the appropriate technology for the job? Take a physical inventory, walking around as you do. Look at more than the computers. Notice everything that plugs into a wall. Which equipment is used, when, and by whom? Notice which pieces are not used. Ask employees in every area why they use or don't use a particular piece of equipment.

Next, take a look at job functions and ask the employees what they think would help them accomplish their jobs more effectively. Ask vendors to present you with new solutions that might answer any unmet needs of your staff.

> The only limit to our realization of tomorrow will be our doubts of today.
>
> —*Franklin D. Roosevelt*

Remember to look at resources beyond the computer. For example, many of your staff members might be more productive if they used a hand-held computer or a personal digital assistant. You don't have to purchase one for everyone, just for those who are willing to use it efficiently and those who would profit by having one. Some of your reluctant users might do better with one of the writing pads that let you take notes on a regular tablet, then move the notes to the computer. If someone is better at dictation than at note taking, encourage them to use a voice-to-text program. Remember, the key is the appropriateness of the technology, not the quantity of technology you have.

One of the most neglected areas of technology is the network. Many companies are only using their networks to share printers or to connect to the Internet. Instead, consider the network as the conduit of information. Employees in multiple areas of the company often work with the same information. With a network, they can share this information. Instead of two people maintaining the same information, they can share the work and free time for other tasks. Be sure to ask employees how they use the network and if they can imagine other ways that the network might be helpful to them. The network will become even more important as we address other issues, so keep it in mind.

Training Is Critical to Your Success

Although you can learn to use technology on your own, it's more fun when you learn with others. Therefore, I will always suggest that you provide some of the technology training in a face-to-face format. This accomplishes several things.

- First, it provides a needed change of pace. People learn better and faster when they are not contending with their daily pressures and tasks. So provide a true change for them. Suggest they have a casual day when they attend training. Provide a barbecue lunch on the lawn. Play a game. Make the learning of technology fun.
- Second, if people have fun while learning to use the technology, they are more likely to look forward to the next learning experience. With technology changing as fast as it does, an open attitude about learning new programs is a must. Start fostering this attitude of fun early in your training program.

- Third, there is a group cohesiveness that is created in face-to-face training. This cohesiveness can provide the basis for ongoing support for group members. This is enhanced even more through the use of online discussions where class members can continue to ask questions and give each other answers, even after the class ends. This type of support cuts down the demand on your help desk and makes end users more independent.

> Our children know more than we do about strategic innovation.
>
> —*Don Tapscott, 1999*

In addition to face-to-face training, you need to provide new learning in continuous formats. This can include tips, just-in-time training, and online courses. Tips can be sent via e-mail, on calendar pages, or in tips booklets. One of the most effective follow-up methods for training that I use is weekly e-mails following a course. For the next 12 weeks, participants get a reminder each week. These reminders use content that was taught in the course. Participants have one of three reactions to these e-mail reminders:

"Hey, I already knew that. I'm pretty smart."
"Wow, I remember that, but I had forgotten the details."
"Hmmm, that's a new and interesting idea."

In all cases, they feel good about the reminders.

Just-In-Time (JIT) training provides one of the most effective means of learning technology. Consider Web-based JIT training. You're using a word processor and realize that you don't know how to insert a graphic. You click on the JIT icon, which leads to the Web page for that program. You search for "graphic" and find the tutorial on inserting a graphic. Not only does it tell you how to do it (which the Help program could have done), but it also shows you a short video on the process and provides links to several graphics locations on your own network. The advantage of Just-In-Time training is that it provides the learning you need, when you need it. It seizes the perfect "teachable moment."

Although face-to-face training is fun and Just-In-Time training may be the fastest and best for retention, online learning may prove to be the most practical in the long run. Using online courses, most of us will be learning at our desks. We have a choice of full courses or individual lessons. The content for online courses runs the gamut of topics from technology to sales to customer service to interviewing. There are courses you can complete on CD-ROM, as well as on the Internet. Some of these courses provide scenarios and let you practice your side of the conversation, even recording your voice. When you're finished with a module, you take a test and the score is sent to your manager, indicating you have completed the training. Online courses have the advantage of providing content on your schedule, at your location, yet letting you still complete courses needed for certification, licensure, and accreditation. They save travel costs for the company, as well as the lost time you might spend traveling.

One final aspect of training is attitude. It is important to foster a "learning as an adventure" attitude in those who use technology. Regardless of what they learn this week, it will be replaced and upgraded next week. They need to learn to take that in stride. The attitude of fun you create in your face-to-face training can help. And learning concepts rather than commands can go a long way toward promoting flexibility in end users. With the concepts of word processing, for example, all they have to ask when they get a new program is "What is the same? What is different?" from the last program they had.

Time: Is There Ever Enough?

With all the training techniques now available, the factor that is obviously missing is time. You need time to attend courses, time to take courses at your desk, time to learn new techniques while you still produce your work. Most of all, you need to provide time for your staff to learn the new techniques. Do not expect them to be experts overnight.

One of the most effective ways of handling this is by setting time-based standards for technology skills. These should be customized to the job tasks and the needs of each employee. For example, an administrative assistant may need to know a word processing program, an e-mail program, and how to fax from the desktop. You will choose the list of skills for each program, then assign a timeline for each skill. This provides a road map of the skills to be learned and the approximate time it will take to learn them. This also gives the assistant's manager a good idea of what skills can be expected when, reducing the possibility of misunderstanding.

The same could apply to a new salesperson. She might need to know how to use her personal digital assistant, how to coordinate her information with the company database, and how to dictate letters on the digital recorder that is later connected to the desktop in the office. Learning each of these skills takes time. During that time, the sales manager needs to know that productivity may not be as high as anticipated for the long run. However, allowing the salesperson time to learn to use the tools appropriately and efficiently will add to long-term productivity. Just give them time.

> This device appeals at once to the eye and ear and naturally forms the habit of attention, which is so difficult to form by the study of books. Whenever a pupil does not understand, the device will have the opportunity of enlarging and making it intelligible.
>
> —*Teacher & Blackboard, 1855*

Team Support: The Oft Overlooked Ingredient

As your technology grows, so should your support structure. Not only do you need technicians who can repair the equipment, but you also need managers who can plan on a long-term basis. Your network administrator, for example, should be familiar with how the business works and should be able to suggest network enhancements that improve the way business is conducted. Here is where you can maximize that investment in your network.

Here, too, is where that investment in face-to-face training and group cohesiveness will begin to provide a return on your investment. Although you still need a "help desk" to answer technical questions, many of the questions will be answered in the groups who trained together or who talk around the coffeepot. This informal support network is important to your long-term goals of technology implementation.

In addition to the people involved in support, consider your investment in the technology. For example, a well run intranet (an internal network that looks like the Internet) will provide the forms and documents your business needs. It will be the basis for much of your Just-In-Time training or online courses that are specific to your company. Support might also be in the form of contracts with other companies that can provide the needed services more affordably and effectively than you can in-house.

The 4 Ts—technology, training, time, and team support—make up the first line of critical attack for taming the technology. When you are confident in those systems you are ready to move to the next line of defense, the 4 Ps.

Plans Provide the Base for Long-Term Growth

If you were starting a company today, you would start with a plan. But the reality is, most people need to get on with the business of the business and don't always take the time to prepare a plan for technology. If that's the case for you, now is the time to do it.

What should you include in your plan? You want to align the mission of the technology with the mission of the company. Next, set out long-term (three years) goals for technology. And finally put these goals into operational terms on a three-year basis, with checkpoints every six months.

Topics should include what you are going to purchase, how you will maintain it, and when and under what circumstances you will repurpose and retire various types of equipment. Next, outline how you will accomplish training for each type of technology. And finally, outline support of each type of equipment. For example, if you plan to purchase laptops for your sales force, you'll want to say who will determine the specifications for the computers, when the laptops will be purchased, and how long you expect them to last. Then you'll need to decide what software programs will be loaded on them, and who and how you will provide the training for them. Finally, you'll need to outline how these laptops will be supported—through an outside vendor or in-house; whether or not the salespeople will be required to bring them in for maintenance; and what procedures you will follow to connect these laptops to the network while the salespeople are on the road.

> Contents change; conduits go on forever
>
> *—Stan Davis and Christopher Meyer from* Blur: The Speed of Change in the Connected Economy

As a last part of your technology plan, you need to include how the use of each technology will be assessed and how the plan will be assessed. You have already identified the skills needed by various job functions and the skills for each software program and piece of equipment. These should be attached to the plan. You should also state how you will determine the successful completion of the skill checkpoints. And finally, you need to set checkpoints for the technology plan itself so that you will know when you have been successful.

Policies Protect Your Culture and Environment

There are three major policies that all companies need to have in place in order to use technology effectively. The first is an Acceptable Use Policy (AUP). This policy states who can use the equipment and for what purpose. AUPs are used widely in order to delineate appropriate use of the Internet by employees. Although there are numerous models of AUPs on the Internet, I always suggest that you consult your lawyer when creating an AUP. Employees should sign a copy of the AUP, so that everyone is very clear about how company equipment is to be used.

Here are just some of the issues that should be covered by an AUP:

- Can an employee use company equipment for personal gain? For example, can she keep the records for her part-time consulting business on a company computer? Can she write a book on her breaks?
- Can an employee use company equipment for personal items? For example, can she send her holiday e-mail newsletter to her friends? Can she subscribe to a joke e-mail newsletter? What if she does it in her spare time or after work?
- What is considered inappropriate use of company equipment? For example, reports suggest that fully 15 percent of the time employees spend on the Internet at work is spent looking at adult sites. Is this appropriate use? Another 14 percent of their time was spent shopping. Is this appropriate?

The second policy that should be in place is a copyright policy. This should state the company's position on copyright and the use of copyrighted materials within the company. It should also outline the specific procedures that employees are to follow in obtaining copyright permission from others. A copyright officer for the company should be named.

Finally, since we live in an information age, you need to have an intellectual property policy in place. This will outline who owns creations, how those creations are protected, and an appeal process for change of ownership.

Procedures Make You More Productive

Once your technology plan is written and your policies have been put in place, you need to concentrate on procedures. This goes beyond the procedures of how to do a job. Rather, with technology, you want to concentrate on replicable processes. These are things that are done on a repetitive basis. If you are able to standardize and create a faster method for doing these tasks, you can add to the level of productivity and recapture some of the "promise of technology."

Here's an example. All of your sales staff does presentations, using computer-based slides. Employ a graphic artist to create several backgrounds that can be used in the slides. Use a multimedia producer to create sound and video clips that can be used in sales presentations. Use a team of your best sales presenters to create at least three sets of slides. Put all of the backgrounds, sound and video clips, and the finished slide shows on a CD-ROM and on your company network or your intranet. Finally, bring in your sales force for a half-day training on how to use the new resources, how to get them from the CD or the intranet, how to edit them, and most importantly, how to deliver them in a meaningful and effective manner. You've now created a turnkey solution for all of your sales presentations, but left the individual sales force with enough autonomy to feel comfortable personalizing their presentations.

> I prefer the dreams of the future rather than the history of the past.
>
> —*Thomas Jefferson*

Look around at other areas of your business. Ask employees what they do on a repetitive basis, then create a standard set of templates and procedures that can be easily used. Not only does this save time for your existing employees, but it also cuts training time for new employees.

Promote Ongoing Use

At this point, you've tamed the jungle of technology. You've cut back the encroaching growth and caged the beast. You feel in control again. But how do you maintain that sense of control? Here are five things you want to promote in order to maintain control of the technology.

1. **Make technology fun.** We started this in our face-to-face training programs. Now just continue it. Decide that learning a new piece of software is an adventure. Cut out and share computer humor. Laugh about the stresses we all have because of technology.

2. **Customize your environment.** If you like pale blue flowers, set your desktop pattern to a picture or wallpaper that reflects your taste. Put the programs you use all of the time into your start-up folder. That way they'll open when you start the computer and you won't have to start them, one by one. Don't store your files in the "default" directories. Instead, organize your hard drive to match the files in your file cabinet. Thus, you may have a folder for marketing, one for technology tips, and one for each client. Store documents, Web pages, even e-mail that pertains to these topics in the appropriate folders—both on your hard drive and in your file cabinet.

   Learn to use your calendar and contact manager. Combine your personal and professional appointments and contacts into the same program. That way you can take care of personal information from the office and work information from home. You can schedule appointments as they arise, linking them to the appropriate contact. You can list to-do items while you are talking to a contact, and have the to-do item show up on your calendar. Most of the current programs have those capabilities; you just need to learn to use them.

   Eliminate yellow stickies—except on the computer. There are "sticky" programs you can add to your computer, if you like to keep track of miscellaneous pieces of information. But if it's information relating to a contact, then add that information to the contact's file in your contact management program. If it's a note about a topic, put it in a word processing document and file it in the electronic folder for that topic.

   Customize your Internet browser. You can change the home page to reflect your interests so that you log into the page each time you start your browser. If you prefer not waiting for the page to download, set your browser to not load a home page. Instead, it will wait for you to tell it which URL to check.

If you track a lot of Internet-based information, consider using one of the "push" technologies that you can customize. With an application like this, you subscribe to the information you want to receive. Then each time you ask it to update, it will provide current information on the topics of your choice. Many companies are now creating Web pages that can be broadcast through these push browsers.

> By 1855 telegraph wires had already made us a networked nation. Until then, communication could only move at the speed of transportation. But the telegraph made the distinction between communication and transportation.
>
> —*David Thornberg, Ph.D., 1999*

3. **Invest in tools.** Now, I'm not saying you need to go out and buy the latest and greatest. But don't be afraid to try new tools as they seem to apply to you. And don't just consider new technology. It's okay to use old technology. I'm using a PDA that is now obsolete. I've looked at the newer models, but I don't need their capabilities; instead, I need exactly what I have. Likewise, with my home copier. I cannot tell you how many crises have been averted by having a copier at home. It's not fancy, but it copies documents, important papers, permission slips, newsletters, and homework very well.

4. **Give yourself permission to say "uncle."** "Uncle," as you will recall, was what we said when we were kids and we'd had enough. That same phenomenon occurs with technology. Sometimes, you just don't want to check your voicemail or answer the phone. Sometimes you want to draw on paper instead of on the computer. Sometimes you want to go somewhere where beepers and cell phones don't work. So tell yourself, "Yes, it's okay to read a book that doesn't have a Web site."

It's okay to take a long weekend and not take your laptop. It's okay not to pick up messages on the weekend. You need to have time when you remember what life was like before technology became a part of it. The long-term survivors in the technology world do that. They withdraw, regroup, and come back for more—with more enthusiasm.

5. **Keep on learning.** We've known for more than 30 years that lifelong learning was an attitude that contributed to a longer life. In today's society it is a necessity, both personally and professionally. Make technology an ongoing part of that learning. Buy a videotape to learn a new program. Tune into PC TV to see new programs and Web sites. Attend a seminar on how to use technology. Take an online course, either to learn new skills or as preparation for an advanced degree. Just keep learning. And remember to have fun while you're doing it!

Congratulations! You've made it through the jungle relatively unscathed. You've set up the systems you will need in order to keep your technology under control. And you've taken steps to foster the attitudes and learning that you and your staff need to stay excited about the changes we face on a daily basis. You've tamed the technology!

ACTION STEPS FOR TAMING TECHNOLOGY

1. Take an inventory of your office technology. Is it appropriate technology for the job?
2. Provide technology training that increases efficiency and makes learning an adventure.
3. Allow the time to learn it right.
4. Promote opportunities for team support.
5. Create a long-term technology plan with short-term checkpoints and assessment criteria..
6. Put in place these three policies: Acceptable Use Policy (AUP), copyright policy, and intellectual property policy.
7. Maximize technology by implementing standards and procedures for all repetitive processes used in your business.
8. Maintain control of your technology, customize to meet your needs, and keep on learning.

About the Author

Jeanette S. Cates, Ph.D., is the CEO of TechTamers, a training and consulting firm based in Austin, Texas. Known as "The Technology Tamer," she is a technology implementation expert who works with organizations that want to use their technology more profitably and with decision makers who want to cut their learning time. Jeanette has developed more than 200 workshops and launched successful technology programs for many multinational corporations as well as for solo entrepreneurs. She is a master of the multimedia presentation and has a proven ability to explain complex concepts in an easy-to-understand manner.

Jeanette S. Cates, Ph.D.
TechTamers
10502 Hardrock
Austin, TX 78750
Phone: (512) 219-5653
Fax: (512) 219-5654
E-mail: *cates@techtamers.com*
Web site: *www.JeanetteCates.com*

Training: Your Competitive Edge

NANCY HANCOCK WILLIAMS, MBA
Management Consultant and Trainer

Don't just sit there, *learn* something!

OK, OK. As a fellow businesswoman, I know you're not *just sitting* at all! Quite the opposite! We're all frantically scurrying around, aren't we, trying to keep up with our hectic schedules. But that's the point. Being this busy, we have a tendency to cling to routines—*don't add one more thing to my agenda, please!*—and so we miss opportunities to make improvements that could allow us to be much, much more successful.

Over the years, I've learned that forcing myself to acknowledge when I need to acquire new knowledge or skill has been one of the most important keys to my success in the business world. And during those times when I've managed a staff it has been equally important to cultivate the ability to notice when *employees* need training, and to take immediate action to provide it.

What works, I've discovered, is to adopt a *training mindset*. By training I don't necessarily mean you should drop everything and rush out to take the next seminar that comes along, or go get an MBA, or, if you're a boss, shell out hundreds of dollars to send your employees to a course or conference.

> Real learning occurs after you think you know it all.
>
> **—Earl Nightingale**

Rather, "training," as I define it, is any sort of formal program by which we (1) identify what's wrong in our or our employees' work life (or what's missing, hard, frustrating, or slowing us down); (2) analyze the knowledge/skill deficiencies that are part of the problem; (3) design specific learning experiences to overcome them; and (4) implement and enjoy the gratifying results.

The emphasis is really on the word *formal*. Formal means you don't just learn on the fly, or get partway through a subject and then quit, or read the material but fail to remember or use it. It means, rather, that you deliberately set out to master a well conceived list of specific topics or skills. The learning can be via any designated method, be it seminar, coaching, reading, conference, or audio/visual session. Formal, as opposed to informal, training is thorough, comprehensive, and *targeted* to the specific knowledge/skill deficiency.

The Training Mindset in Action

To understand this concept better, perhaps what we should do first is define what a training mindset is *not*. Have you heard any statements like the following?

- "I wish I could get this spreadsheet done faster. I bet there's some trick to copying and formatting these cells. But I'm on a deadline so I better just plod along doing everything manually."

- "I'm just so nervous when I have to speak in front of a group. I can't sleep the night before, and I have no idea how to prepare so it comes off smoothly."
- "I'm in a fog about these new products. I keep getting so confused about the specifications that my customers look skeptical when I try to explain them."

The individual with a training mindset would never accept these statements at face value. She would hear herself saying them, and recognize each of them as a signal that it's time to stretch her wings.

Let's take the first example and apply our guidelines for formal training to it.

1. **Identify what's wrong.** Listen to your gut. What are you saying to yourself? *"I'm slow as molasses on this spreadsheet! If this is all this software can do, it's a pretty pitiful tool!"* Next, assess the truth of what you're feeling, and compare it to other similar situations. *"Realistically, would this software have sold so well if it was this limited? No. Probably what's going on is that I'm not even using 10 percent of what it has to offer."*

2. **Identify the knowledge/skill deficiencies.** Find or develop a compendium of what there is to know on this subject, and use it as a checklist to determine what your deficiency is. For example, the spreadsheet program probably came with a manual. Flipping through it to note what the program can do— that you don't yet know how to do—will generate your checklist.

   > It's not what you know when you start. It's what you learn and put to good use.

3. **Design specific learning experiences.** With a computer skills deficiency, you could take a course. Often this is an effective solution. I recommend getting yourself on the mailing list for all commercial, college, or extension programs in your town so when learning deficiencies become apparent—in computers or any other

subject—you can consult the available courses first. However, remember that courses, seminars, and other "outside" programs aren't by nature *targeted* to your unique needs. They're usually best for gaining a broad background in a particular subject.

In my career, I've often found that my own self-training methods are more effective. In this case, I would decide to work late two or three evenings and force myself to wade through material (e.g., three chapters in the manual) that addresses my area of deficiency. The important thing with self-study is not to try to "find" the time, but to make the time.

4. **Implement.** Running your own training program takes discipline—something I personally am in short supply of! So I have to coddle myself. In the spreadsheet case, I would block out the time on my calendar, just as if I were going to a class, and buy myself something tasty for dinner. Then I'd repair to my desk and, with the office largely empty of distracting fellow workers, comb through the chapters. I find my motivation can be aided by comparing the hours I am devoting to training to the excess time I am likely to spend on my next spreadsheet if I don't do the training. A reward when I'm done can also be effective. A slice of rich chocolate cake really motivates me!

I have also found that there are certain techniques that help me further master the material: (1) finding a project on which to use the new skills immediately; (2) teaching the material to someone else in the near future (if you're a boss, teach it to your staff, and if not, brag about it to coworkers so they will come to you!); and (3) preparing crib sheets and visual aids to keep close to my computer for reference. Figure out what your preferred learning time frame is—on something like a computer program, some people would rather learn a little bit each night for several

> Excellence is an art won by training and habituation.
>
> *—Aristotle*

weeks. That doesn't work for me—I prefer a "blitz" reminiscent of the all-nighters I used to pull in college! *Do whatever works for you.*

These steps help you adopt a training mindset in nearly all situations. Now let's look at the other two statements we started out with. In the case where the individual is made ill by having to make a speech, clearly assessing what's wrong is essential to appropriate relief from the pain! For example, if you determine that what really makes you nervous is being unskilled in how to prepare and deliver a speech, then hiring a speech coach or taking an intensive one-day workshop might be a fast solution.

> Learn by doing. There is no substitute for experience and no finer teacher.
>
> —*Mary-Ellen Drummond*

However, if you determine that the problem isn't knowledge, but rather just raw irrational fear, then you might need something long-term and continuous to work it out of your system, such as joining a Toastmasters club (an international public speaking organization, which I can personally recommend after five years as a member). Because ferreting out the real problem can be difficult when you're emotionally tied up in knots, one way to be sure you're doing it accurately is to talk out the problem with another person who can help maintain objectivity for you. *Important: don't jump to the solution until you have completed the assessment in steps 1 and 2!*

In the other statement earlier, where the individual was unclear about the products she was selling, if her company offers a course that might be one route to clarity. However, it is not as targeted or efficient as self-study. And so often, I see employees just waiting around for their company to "give" them training, like baby birds with their mouths open. Successful people in my experience don't wait—they go out and get or create the training for themselves. In this case, once this businesswoman has identified exactly what she's missing, she might elect to go talk to the designers to get a more in-depth explanation of the specifications, or sit down with all the product literature and memorize it, or draw a graph on a big sheet of paper contrasting one product's specifications with another so she can see them laid out in visual form, or create a series of explanations and rehearse them with a fellow salesperson who also needs to present them more cogently.

Your Competitive Advantage

Developing the capacity to go out and get your own training can mean the difference between being perceived as *good* at what you do, or absolutely *terrific* at it. It is important to remember that we all have different ways of processing information and learning. Researchers tell us that some of us are "auditory" learners (we remember best what we hear), some "visual" (we remember what we see), and some "kinesthetic" (we need to move, talk, or *feel* the information in order to remember it). In my experience, very few people are auditory, and the rest of us are either visual or kinesthetic. I've found that using a variety of media—attacking the information in several different ways—works best for mastering it.

> What I hear I forget.
> What I see I remember.
> What I do I understand.
>
> —*Confucius*

I've discovered a number of tools that help cement concepts in my mind. Both the preparation of these tools and the enthusiastic use of them act as learning aids. Here are just a few that have worked for me:

- Handwritten flashcards to use when I'm jogging—colored pens can further help.
- A large handmade collage poster (pictures and words) for my bathroom mirror so I can study a limited number of concepts while I dry my hair.
- Writing specifications over and over in a notebook until I memorize them.
- Self-recorded audiotapes that I can play—and talk back to—in my car.
- Pretending to be a teacher of the subject and "lecturing" (out loud) at the wall of my bedroom at home. (My husband thinks I'm crazy!)

- Drawing colored pictures or headlines (the act of drawing in color seems to "set" information in my head better).
- Dancing and shouting the material. I'm serious! I can remember the first class I took in accounting (not particularly my forte, but necessary for a business career). On my daily jogs, I'd hop, skip, leap, jump, and yell "Assets equal liabilities plus owner equity!" into the wind—and that was how the Fundamental Accounting Equation got sunk into my unwilling brain!

I want to say a word here about *memorization* as a tool for achieving mastery. Memorization, or "rote learning," went so far out of favor a couple of decades ago that many of us feel it's heretical even to mention it. Hogwash! Even when dealing with highly conceptual or complex material, memorization can give you a *toehold*, a foundation on which to build further knowledge. Most of us can't just read or hear something once and remember it. So a lot of my learning tools involve full memorization.

When You're Managing Others

Having a training mindset can be even more critical if you're managing a department or running your own business. After all, you're trying to accomplish much larger goals, through other people. And with other people to rely on and coordinate, there's an even greater danger of seeing processes as "fixed" and employees as unchangeable. I overheard this statement from a client recently: "The girls in customer service [a woman CEO said this!] are basically rude and unpolished. Just walk by their desks—you always hear them just yelling at customers. I think we're going to have to replace most of them."

This kind of sentiment—especially if you hear yourself saying it—should immediately raise a red flag. Let's look at this situation in depth. The expense of firing and replacing experienced workers is *enormous*. Putting

> All of us look for people who can make us better, stronger, wiser.
>
> —*Oprah Winfrey*

together a couple of days of training—that you conduct yourself or hire someone else to deliver—can save tens of thousands of dollars and will likely retain at least 50 percent of the workers. In my experience it's more like 90 percent. In this case, I insisted that my client look at training solutions first.

Our initial step was, of course, to *identify the problem*. When working with a group of people, the identification process must be based on fact, not assumption. I spent a day observing the agents on the phone, interviewing them to find out what their frustrations were, and understanding the department's objectives. What I found was that the work processes were not clear, so the agents fumbled around a lot, irritating the customers and causing them to yell at the agents. The agents had no training in how to handle tense interactions and were miserable fighting it out with customers all the time. What I also found out was that, contrary to the CEO's assumption, every single agent was desperate to learn what to do and to make their job work better. With perhaps one exception, they were not inherently rude people!

> The essence of real leadership is to allow your people to see **your** need and desire for learning.
>
> —*Jack Kahl*

Once we knew what was going on, we were able to be methodical in constructing a *list of knowledge deficiencies* and prioritizing them. With this particular client, I pulled together a committee of individuals in the group and let them do the analysis. Another technique is to scan the literature and professional journals in the functional area and create a list of topics that would contribute to better performance if mastered. In this case, we determined that a program on dealing with emotional customers, clarifying processes, and filling in the gaps in the agents' systems knowledge would be the most targeted approach.

Now that we understood the problem, we were in a position to *design the training*. This particular client was on a tight budget. So we designed the program ourselves! The local library was a great resource for video and audiocassettes, workbooks, articles, and books on the subject. I used a great reference book I own on corporate games and training exercises. In about six hours we put together a program that included a variety of media (watching videos, listening to audiotapes, brief lectures, exercises, worksheets, and lots of time to actually practice the appropriate interactions and scripts).

> You can't learn anything from experiences you're not having.
>
> —*Louis L'Amour*

It never fails. As you implement the course, you see the light bulbs flashing on in people's heads. Our goal in this program wasn't to have the agents simply understand the *theory* of dealing with difficult customers, but to actually *do* it. We wanted them not only to *understand* the processes and the computer, but be able to *apply* their skills. Thus, we made sure most of our class time was spent on doing and applying. The results were incredible. Out of 12 agents, only two didn't take the training to heart and had to be replaced. The other 10 went right out and began practicing their new skills, and customer complaints dropped by more than 80 percent within three months.

Illustrating one of my pet peeves, here's another example of how a *training mindset* can make all the difference. In a typical office scenario we have a brand-new employee who's just come on board, but no one has made a clear and professional plan for imparting to her the knowledge she needs to get up and running and focused in her job. She spends her first week, month, or even year being half as productive as she could be. This makes no business sense whatsoever. So I advocate that all new employees be given a specific and focused training protocol to ensure that they learn their entire job as quickly and efficiently as humanly possible. Here's an example:

TRAINING SCHEDULE FOR JANICE NEWPERSON, CUSTOMER SERVICE ASSOCIATE I

DATE	TIME	ACTION	PURPOSE	PERSON RESPONSIBLE
Mon., 3/12	8–8:30	Tour building	Meet everyone in department and learn location of copier, restrooms, etc.	Peter Jones, supervisor
	8:30–9	Meeting with George Henning, division manager	Company overview	Peter
	9–9:30	Meeting with Kathleen Parr, department manager	Division and department overview	Peter
	9:30–11	HR orientation	Watch company video, discuss benefits, employee handbook overview	Marcia Smith, division HR specialist
	11–12	Team meeting	Attend weekly Team Meeting with immediate coworkers	Peter
	12–1	Lunch at Checkos	Informal lunch with coworkers	Paula Neman and Betty Lang
	1–3	Tutorial with Melissa Parrish, product manager	Overview of Group I products, specifications	Peter
	3–5	Observation of CS agent	Listen in on phone ordering process	Paula Neman
Tues., 3/13	8–12	Tour of testing lab	Understand how Group I products are designed and tested	Susan Browner, lab tech
	12–1	Lunch	Coworkers are available to join you	
	1–5	Group 1 product self-study	Complete Group I Product workbook and quiz	Peter
Wed., 3/14	8–10	Observation of CS agent	Listen in on phone ordering process	Peter
	10–12	Read systems manual	Understand structure of the PETARC system	Peter
	12–1	Lunch		
	1–4	Computer Training 1A (in Building H12)	First of 10 three-hour sessions	Horace Jensen, MIS training coordinator
	4–5	Discussion/touch base	Review learning so far and discuss any issues	Peter

Note: Most training protocols should cover *at least* the employee's first month.

Research on adult lifelong learning has consistently shown that adults who deliberately seek out learning throughout their lives stay more mentally fresh, more alert, and more enthusiastic about life than people who fall back on what they already know and get stuck in routine and sameness. In the business world, a commitment to continuous, focused learning is what I call the *training mindset*. It makes sense that we can become more nimble, tough, and skilled business competitors by cultivating a training mindset and making ongoing training integral to our professional activities. No matter how busy I get, I remind myself daily that any investment in my own or my employees' training is my competitive advantage and my key to success!

> Life is my college. May I graduate well and earn some honors.
>
> **—Louisa May Alcott**

10 ACTION STEPS TO SUCCESS

1. Get on the mailing list for every college, extension, evening program, and commercial seminar company in your area so you can stay abreast of local training availability.

2. Subscribe to professional training journals (*Training, Performance Management, American Society for Training and Development Journal*) so you can get on the mailing lists for nationwide seminar companies and training resource firms.

3. If you have access to a corporate library, check out its services now. Also obtain library cards for the public library closest to your work, and for any local university libraries as feasible.

4. Learn how to conduct research on the Internet—it can be a great source of training solutions and ideas.

5. Cultivate a training mindset in yourself and your employees.

6.   Figure out now what your learning style and skill-building time frame are, and henceforward use them as guidelines when you plan your self-study. When designing employee training, plan to accommodate many learning styles and time frames.

7.   Don't get used to frustration in your work—feel it, and heed the signal to figure out what's fundamentally wrong.

8.   Avoid assumptions about performance deficiencies—be sure you get all the facts before designing or purchasing training or arriving at irrevocable solutions such as terminating employees.

9.   Take a multimedia approach—we learn best when information is presented to us in a variety of ways.

10.   Keep track of your results—you'll be amazed at the improvement you initiated!

About the Author

Nancy Hancock Williams, a principal in her own management consulting practice, specializes in service process re-engineering, management development, and custom training solutions for small and large businesses. She previously was vice president of operations at Ariat International, Inc., a fast-growing equestrian footwear start-up. Prior to that she spent nine years at Wells Fargo Bank, where she held several positions including vice president of operations for the small business lending division and vice president and regional manager of a territory of 20 retail branches and more than 350 employees. She holds a BA from the University of California, San Diego, and an MBA from Stanford University.

Nancy H. Williams, MBA
1167 Laureles Drive
Los Altos, CA 94022
Phone: (650) 941-7872
E-mail: *nancywil@ix.netcom.com*

chapter fourteen

The Art of Getting Referrals

GAYLENE PRINGLE
Founder, The Leadership Edge

When I started The Leadership Edge in 1989, I knew very little about the training and development field. My background was in high-technology sales and sales management. What I lacked in industry knowledge, I made up for in passion, values, and a clarity and commitment to creating a great company that served others while supporting my life and dreams. I had a passion for learning, business, people, and creative problem solving. I knew that my vision for my life was to be a catalyst for empowering people worldwide to continually make positive changes in their personal and professional lives. These passions, combined with a highly entrepreneurial family background, made starting my own business in this industry a perfect fit. Except for two problems: I had no clients and no track record. But I did have a dream list, relationships with great people, and the knowledge that the best way to create that ideal business was through referrals. If I could begin with a handful of great people and provide an outstanding program to them, I believed they would begin to spread the word. The amazing thing was, it worked! Today we have more than 3,000 clients who can all be traced back to the original 10 participants in my first class.

Why Referrals?

One referral call is the equivalent of 12 cold calls. When I started my business, I didn't want to be focused on activity, i.e., making a hundred cold calls a day; I wanted to focus on results. The referral process was key to this. Today, the phone rings at least three times a week with another referral. After 10 years of working the referral process, the results are effortless. I do no outbound marketing today, and yet my business continues to grow at a steady rate with high-quality opportunities.

Referrals build relationships. When someone (referral source) refers you to someone else (referral), it strengthens your relationship with them (referral source). You are thankful for the referral. It has saved you a tremendous amount of time and increased your profitability. From their perspective, they are happy to have the opportunity to do something great for you.

> Referrals allow you to maintain a higher quality and extremely profitable client base.
>
> —*Gaylene Pringle*

In addition, the relationship between your referral source and the person being referred is strengthened; your referral source cared enough to help solve a problem for him/her, saving time for the referred party, while dramatically reducing the risks associated with selecting a vendor.

Finally, the relationship between you and the referral begins with a high level of trust, enabling you to quickly understand the referral's needs and diagnose whether or not you are the best solution for them.

Referrals allow you to service rather than sell. There are very few individuals who feel more comfortable selling than they do servicing a client's needs. When you approach a new prospect as the result of a referral, you enter into the relationship with a much higher degree of trust and therefore, influence.

You've Got to Earn It!

Don't worry. I don't believe that you should ask for referrals at every opportunity. We need to earn the right to ask. I believe the referral process should always build relationships, never alienate friends and associates, and always result in everyone winning. It's not that tough. You just need the three "must haves" to make this process a success.

Here are the three "must haves":

1. People with influence as referral sources
2. "I'll do anything for you" relationships with your top referral sources
3. Educated referral sources

With these simple principles at work, you will never hear a "No" when asking for referrals. Asking for referrals will actually become something that is easy and no longer uncomfortable for you. You will receive very qualified new business prospects, you will have stronger relationships, and you will have fun!

People with Influence

Your top referral sources must have influence. It doesn't mean they have to be the mayor, a CEO, or someone with a prominent title. Rather, they must be people who have influence with your ideal prospect. Without influence and respect, the referral is meaningless. Before you can identify "people of influence" to assist you as referral sources, you need to be clear on who your ultimate prospect is.

Who is your ideal prospect? Think for a moment about the type of person whom you are best positioned to serve. Make a list that includes answers to the following questions: What size company are they? Where are they located? What industry are they in? Why would they need you? Who in the company is your ideal contact?

Now, we want to add to this list the types of people who tend to select you or your firm. What do they value? Who do they feel most comfortable with? Do they want someone who will educate or advise them? Will they prefer someone who has a sense of humor or someone who is more to the point and direct? Do they view their vendors as partners in business? Are they looking for the least expensive solution, or are they willing to pay for quality? Think about the psychographics, i.e., the kinds of people who would choose you. Add these characteristics to your list.

> The process builds stronger relationships and, best of all, positions you to be your best, resulting in even more referrals.

From all of the characteristics on your ideal prospect list, prioritize the "critical five." These top five characteristics are what you will share with your referral sources when they ask you to define your ideal prospect. By limiting the criteria to five, you will be succinct and to the point. For example, my company specializes in executive, management, and advanced sales training and development. My critical five characteristics are:

- CEO or high-level human resource professional
- High-growth, entrepreneurial company
- Have demonstrated a commitment to their people and value their people, i.e., they have on-site day care, great benefits, exercise programs, etc.
- Have invested in training programs in the past
- Have a highly educated population who is not typically educated in business, or individuals who have new responsibilities for which they were not trained, i.e., scientists who now must manage, or attorneys and accountants who are now responsible for business development

Identifying Untapped Sources for Referrals

Did you know that 80 percent of clients would be willing to refer business, and yet only 20 percent are ever asked? That means that 60 percent of your client base is just waiting, waiting to send you prosperity, growth, and fun! Your past and current clients are a great place to start when you are looking for potential referral sources. They know you, believe in you, and have the confidence that you will solve real problems for their friends, clients, and associates. But even though this source of referrals can prove to be incredibly successful for you, you may find yourself needing additional referral sources.

> Referrals build relationships; they allow you to service your client rather than sell.

Research has shown that most people have influence over approximately 200 people. In discovering your best referral sources, you want to identify the fewest number of people who have the greatest number of your ideal prospects in their sphere of influence. For example, if you were a CPA for a large firm, your critical five characteristics of your ideal prospect might be:

- The CEO or CFO of the largest companies in your market
- The CEO or CFO of companies in your targeted industry
- The CEO or CFO of a company facing rapid growth and on the verge of going into international markets
- The CEO or CFO who appreciates creativity, innovation, and direct, bottom-line advice
- The CEO or CFO who values quality and is willing to pay for it, as evidenced by her high-profile (and high-fee) attorneys and investment advisers

To begin identifying your top referral sources, those people who can lead you to your ideal prospect, you might ask yourself the following questions:

Who else sells to this market?
- Estate planners
- High-end attorneys
- Anyone who sells products with a very high purchase price
- Investment bankers
- Consultants
- Executive coaches

Do I know anyone in these fields? Do I have alumni who could interact with my ideal prospect?
- Neighbors?
- Vendors?
- Religious affiliations?
- Past clients?
- Current clients?
- Prospects?

Begin to list the names of individuals who come to mind. Regardless of how strong or weak your relationships might be, write them down.

Next, rate their level of influence with your ideal prospects on a scale of 1–5, 1 representing "not influential" and 5 representing "very influential."

> Think first of how you can give to others. In the best case you will receive many referrals; in the worst case you will dramatically in-crease client retention.

You will want to focus your effort and energy on those referral sources who have the greatest degree of influence with your ideal prospects: those with a rating of 3 or greater. Influence is something that is difficult to create for others and often takes a tremendous amount of time for an individual to develop. You, therefore, use this as your first criterion in prioritizing your referral sources.

If you do not have referral sources who have high levels of influence with your ideal prospects, you will apply the referral process to finding and developing more influential sources. You would begin by listing your ideal prospect—in this case, the characteristics of your ideal referral source. You would then apply the questions just listed to identify individuals who can make the appropriate introductions to these more influential individuals.

Developing the "I'll Do Anything for You" Relationship

The second "must have" is a great relationship with your top referral sources. When you ask for a referral, you are asking people to make an effort on your behalf. They have to be enthusiastic fans of yours and have the desire to help you. Before you ever ask for this help, I believe you need to earn the right. I believe in the philosophy of giving. By this I don't mean giving just so you get something back, but giving because of the joy it brings to you and others and the wonderful relationships that are created.

> Every account should have a relationship strategy.

Identifying the ways in which we can give to others is not difficult. When I meet with my clients and referral sources, I ask questions, listen, and observe. It is amazing how much you can learn by doing these simple things. When meeting with one of my clients recently, I asked him how his family was doing. He told me that his son was applying to colleges, one of which happened to be my alma mater, the University of Pennsylvania. I asked him if I could be of help by writing a letter of recommendation for his son. He was thrilled.

Let me share with you some of the quick and easy things you can do to build stronger relationships with your referral sources.

- While you are reading the paper in the morning read it with one of your referral sources in mind. Are there any articles they would find to be of interest?
- Set up an e-mail group for your referral sources. Periodically touch base with them, sharing tips from a great book or seminar that you attended.

- When you receive a mailer for a great seminar, forward the information on to your referral sources.
- When you read a great book, buy extra copies so that you can give them to your referral sources.
- Call in the evening and leave them a quick voice mail letting them know that you are thinking of them.
- Refer others to them.
- When you go to lunch next time, ask them what their greatest challenges are. Understand their personal and professional goals. See if you have any resources that you can use to assist them.

When you take great care of your clients, associates, and friends you will feel great and have fun. Later, when you need assistance in developing your business, you will never hear a "No." You will not alienate people or create discomfort for anyone. You will have earned the right to ask for help by having served as a valuable resource and a committed friend. The response you can expect is, "I would do anything for you. How can I help?"

If you never ask for referrals, you will still have the joy that giving brings as well as unparalleled client loyalty. If you are in a competitive business where client retention is key (and who isn't?), you can't lose.

Take a moment to go back to the list of referral sources that you generated. Rate each of your sources on the quality of your relationship and their willingness to refer business to you. A rating of 1 represents a "weak relationship and an unwillingness to help." A rating of 5 represents a "strong relationship and a willingness to help." If your ratings are not what you would like them to be, begin to identify the ways in which you can give more to them.

> Dig your well before you're thirsty!
>
> —Harvey Mackay

If They Don't Know What You Do, They Can't Help You

Your third "must have" is referral sources who are ready, willing, and able to help you. Many of your potential referral sources actually know very little about what you do. I have found this to be especially true with women. We tend not to talk a great deal of business with our friends and other sources. We need to change this! If people do not understand what it is you do, they are unlikely to take the risk of referring someone to you.

> Before you meet new people, before you make that call, do your homework. Find that common ground. Determine where their needs and interests lie. Make that connection.

You must educate your clients and referral sources on all that you do. Make certain that they have product literature. Invite them to your client seminars, even if they aren't a client. For example, the CPA we were discussing earlier might invite some high-end insurance agents or attorneys to her seminar. It provides them with an opportunity to learn more about her and her business, as well as to network with their ideal prospects. Make certain that your referral sources are on your press release list. Let them see all of the good news, not just reprints of the articles that the press decided to pick up.

One of my favorite methods of educating our referral sources is through client benefit stories. The next time someone calls you on the telephone and asks how you are, share a client benefit story. Your response might be something like, "I am doing great. I just had the opportunity to save my client more than ten thousand dollars in taxes." Or "I'm great. I am looking forward to meeting with my high-technology client this afternoon to discuss some international taxation issues." When we share a client benefit story, it does two things. First, it lets them know we have a particular kind of client. That is always good. Second, it educates them about the kind of clients that we work with. This very often leads to a referral.

Their response might be, "I didn't know you worked in high technology. Have you met with Joe Smith from Techno Company?"

$$Education = Credibility + Ability$$

Rate your referral sources on their knowledge of your business. A rating of 1 would represent "very little knowledge." A rating of 5 would represent "tremendous knowledge." If your ratings are not what you would like them to be, focus your next interaction with your referral source on educating them about what you do.

Prioritizing Your Referral Sources

Now that you have rated your referral sources against each of your three "must haves," total their ratings for the three categories. Do you have any referral sources whose total rating falls between 13 and 15? These people are ready, willing, and able to refer business to you. Look at their names. You probably would have no problem asking them for a referral, would you? What are you waiting for? Schedule a meeting with them today and begin to share your "critical five" ideal prospect criteria.

> Never, never pass up an opportunity to meet new people. Your antennae should be up your whole life.

For those referral sources whose total score falls below 13, look at those areas where you are weak and focus your time, effort, and energy on implementing some of the ideas that were shared.

You now have the ability to be purposeful in your prospecting efforts. You can approach your referral source without fear, knowing that they would delight in the opportunity to assist you in building your business. You will spend each day positioned to do your best work with people whom you truly enjoy. Your relationships with clients and associates will be stronger, and your reputation will be unparalleled.

The next time your phone rings, you will feel excitement and enthusiasm, knowing that it could bring you your next great client.

PUTTING IT TO WORK:
THE TOP 10 GUIDELINES TO FOLLOW

1. Do *not* ask for referrals at every opportunity!
2. You've got to earn the right to ask.
3. Be clear on what you want. You will get what you ask for.
4. You have the power to choose your clients. Use your "critical five" criteria.
5. Everyone you meet is a prospect, a referral source, or knows someone who is a prospect or referral source.
6. Your strategy: Find the fewest number of people who have the greatest amount of influence and contacts in your target market.
7. Stop, look, listen, and give.
8. Every day you have an opportunity to share a client benefit story and educate your referral sources.
9. Referral prospecting doesn't take a lot of time; it just takes focus.
10. There is no easier, more cost-effective, and efficient way of selling than through referrals—and it's fun!

About the Author

Gaylene Pringle has a passion for assisting people to reach their highest potential. She is founder and president of The Leadership Edge, a training organization that provides leadership, management, and business development programs to executives and managers striving to achieve their highest potential while directing a prospering, innovative business. As a businesswoman, trainer and facilitator, speaker, and published author, she creates and presents custom training programs and keynote speeches to business leaders across the country. She has a national reputation for her unique programs that train scientists, engineers, accountants, and attorneys in corporate leadership, management, and business development.

Gaylene Pringle, Owner
The Leadership Edge
P.O. Box 7203
Rancho Santa Fe, CA 92067
Phone: (760) 436-5678
Fax: (760) 436-5508
E-mail: *Gaylene@TheLeadershipEdge.com*
Web site: *www.TheLeadershipEdge.com*

chapter fifteen

The Rewards of Direct Sales

NANCY SMITH
Executive Director, Creative Memories

In 1990, while going through a personal transition period, I had a conversation with my sister about career possibilities. I was feeling trapped because I could only think of traditional employment alternatives. In her enthusiastic way, my sister invited me to broaden my thinking from "job" to "vocation." "People who are truly successful," she said, "are those who do what they love, make a difference to others, and get paid for it in the process."

At the time, I was a young mother who had left a brief career as a full-time medical sales representative to be home with my children. My primary focus was mothering a six- and a two-year-old. I did take on some part-time work as a substitute teacher to add a small amount to the family finances. During this time a friend and I talked about what it would be like to *really*

> The more clearly some-
> one sees the future, the
> more confidently they
> work in the present.
>
> —*From Dr. Tom
> Barrett's book,* Dare to
> Dream, Work to Win

do what we loved. I laughed and said, "Well, I doubt anyone would pay me to plant tulips or make photo albums!"—naming two of my favorite hobbies.

The next week the same friend brought me a newspaper article. "I saw this and immediately thought of you!" she said. The article featured Diane Wallace, a sales consultant for a company called Creative Memories. She had a business in which she taught others how to make beautiful keepsake scrapbook albums. I have to talk to this woman, I thought. I have to see if this is something that I can do too! That very day I set into motion the start of my own direct sales business, and that decision has affected my life more positively than anything I ever could have imagined.

Find Your Passion

Finding a purpose in life that uses your talents and energy, and has a positive impact on yourself and others, will empower you. When you find work you love, the passion you feel for what you're doing is exhilarating. It helps you visualize and take action on the incredible possibilities life can offer. Have you ever wondered if you are doing what you were meant to do? Have you thought how wonderful it would be to do what you love for a living? Did you think, as many do, that only a lucky few have that luxury? The truth is, you too can make this dream a reality for yourself.

To get started, consider what you're truly enthusiastic about. Examine what experiences in life have had an impact on you. What activities have left you the most satisfied, exhilarated, or proud? These experiences and activities will give you the clues to discovering your true desires. You may not only discover where your passions lie, but expand your thinking into ways to include them in creating your future.

At the Heart of Selling

Having a strong appreciation for the product you work with is an important factor in direct sales success. I didn't have any knowledge about the direct sales industry. In fact, I had very little true sales experience, and I had never run my own business. What I did have was excitement and enthusiasm for sharing my convictions about how wonderful scrapbook albums are. I appreciated how they helped me to record and celebrate what is important to me—my growing children and the many blessings in my life. I loved the products, the colorful pages, the journaling. I created album pages late into the night. I even dreamed about my new business. I enjoyed everything about working with my photos and teaching others how to create albums for themselves.

I knew how much making albums could enrich their lives and I wanted to inspire people to take action. I knew I could strengthen families through my positive message. People in my classes told me that my passion made me very credible when I shared the concept of Creative Memories with them.

> When I look into the future, it's so bright, it burns my eyes.
>
> —*Oprah Winfrey*

At first, I was a little resistant to the idea of being a salesperson. I was afraid I might be seen as pushy. Sales success, I discovered, comes when you put the needs of others first and you truly want what is best for them. In my first classes I shared from my personal experiences and, with excitement, showed my own albums and taught others how to create their own. I soon realized that at the heart of selling is a transfer of enthusiasm as well as the joy of meeting others' needs.

I focused on helping my clients feel inspired and confident in their ability. I asked them questions about what they wanted to accomplish and showed them solutions that my products provided. To my amazement, when I approached people this way, the sales followed. I realized this is how all people experience incredible success in direct sales, whether they are selling cosmetics, cooking equipment, health products, or items for the home.

Perseverance Pays

Starting a business can be a roller coaster of experiences, with many ups and downs. In the first few months the principal way of growing the business in direct sales is having classes, shows, or parties. In this early start-up phase of my business, I crowned myself the "Cancel Queen" because I had six classes cancel in a row. This kind of experience can really shake your confidence. But after the sixth cancellation I decided I wasn't going to quit. I became more determined to succeed.

I was unshakable on this point. The thought of not having this new business that I was so passionate about was more upsetting to me than any challenge that could arise. I learned that one of the keys to success, as your business grows, is perseverance and staying focused on the big picture. You cannot get caught up in the little disappointments along the way. You have to look at what is happening and determine what action you can take that will continue your movement forward.

I learned that if I didn't want to have classes cancel, I would need to strengthen my skills at helping the coordinators be successful by offering them more suggestions on what to tell their friends and giving them materials that would help them get a group excited about attending. Overscheduling was a must. I realized that if I had one or two sessions scheduled and something happened to make a class evaporate, my business prospects were cut in half, which could be devastating. But if I had eight to 10 scheduled, and one canceled, it wasn't a big deal. This principle helped me to be consistent in my booking and selling efforts. I built my business by conducting an average of two events a week, every week, with perseverance. Six months after my run of cancellations I ranked seventh nationally in personal sales. Continuing at the pace of two classes a week, I went on to become number one in sales nationally for two years in a row out of a Creative Memories consultant base of thousands.

> If you think you can, you can, and, if you think you can't, you're right.
>
> —*Mary Kay Ash*

Develop Confidence and Communication Skills

When I first began teaching about Creative Memories, speaking in front of a group of adults was a new experience for me. In fact, my anxiety could have held me back from my eventual successes if I had given in to the fear. I finally made a decision to do something about it after one class in which my face and neck turned beet red and my lips trembled the whole time I spoke.

One of the first action steps I took was to enroll in an eight-week course called "Speech Crafters" by Toastmasters International, a nonprofit educational organization. Members work together to improve their speaking and leadership skills. Eventually, I joined a local Toastmasters club to learn how to overcome my fears and to improve my presentation. I also started reading self-improvement books on communication, sales, and leadership. However, the main key to improving how I felt about talking in front of others was to just do it. I made a point to "feel the fear and do it anyway." With each class my confidence grew, and each time I spoke, it became less and less difficult. In time I found ways to be conversational in my speaking style, even when I spoke to a crowd. People told me they could relate to me easily because I wasn't formal and I was someone who had thoughts and feelings and fears just as they did.

> To be successful, the first thing to do is fall in love with your work.
>
> —*Sister Mary Lauretta*

Over the years I have learned that confidence comes from experience. Experience comes only from jumping in and getting your feet wet. When I was afraid of situations such as making phone calls to prospects, recruiting someone into the business, or giving a speech, I would say to myself, "How would a confident person act in these circumstances?" Then I would make a point to act like a confident person. The simple truth is that somewhere between acting confident and looking confident, you become the assured person you want to be.

Share What You Have Learned and Empower Others

When I started with Creative Memories, I didn't understand that it was a direct sales company, or even what direct sales was about. I wanted to focus on my own business, my customers, and also using the products myself. I didn't really think of how much larger this opportunity could be and where it could lead until I heard Lyn Johnson, a senior director, speak at a Creative Memories convention about the power of collective effort. She asked the thousands of attendees, "Do you love what you do? Do you find satisfaction in your work? Do you find it a blessing in your family?" The attendees enthusiastically answered "Yes!" to each question. Then she asked with tongue-in-cheek humor, "And you don't want to tell other people about it? My, aren't you selfish?" This comment truly struck me.

> Opportunities are usually disguised as hard work, so most people don't recognize them.
>
> —*Ann Landers*

I started my business because I wanted to contribute to making families stronger by teaching people about how positive it is to make family albums. I was experiencing the satisfaction of doing what I loved and making financial gains because of my focus on teaching classes and selling. After hearing Lyn Johnson talk, I was inspired to enrich lives in a bigger way. I realized that I could make a difference with other women. Many people are looking for a way to make their family a priority and still have a business that is rewarding and meets financial needs. I know I want to help other women experience the joy of doing something they love. I was excited to share the tools of personal growth, freedom, and flexibility that a direct sales career brings.

In helping others, my business grew tenfold. What changed for me, as I experienced more recruiting success, was a change in attitude. I stopped worrying about what people might think of me and focused more on seeing potential in others. I tried to recognize skills in people and share a vision with them of how this business could work and enrich their lives. One of my first consultants, Janette Ballard, stated in a letter, "I don't know what prompted you to ask me about doing Creative Memories as a business, but I'll always be glad you did. Your friendship and Creative Memories have impacted my life so positively."

> You have to be willing to step out of the pack and take risks, even jump completely out of your element if that's what it takes.
>
> —*Carol Bartz*

I taught others to have a business like my own and set an example to include recruiting as part of their business effort. Last year alone my unit of three lines of consultants generated over $5 million in sales for Creative Memories. The ability to expand your vision to include the dreams of others can make you all that much more successful. I love this quote by Zig Ziglar: "You can get everything you want in life, if you just help enough other people get what they want."

Set Goals and Make an Action Plan to Achieve Them

Experts say you are 10 times more likely to achieve a goal if you write it down, yet most people resist writing down what they want to accomplish. Many people hold back from goal setting because they fear they will fail to achieve the goals they set or they don't know how to set goals. My approach was to determine a goal, and then break it down into the individual action steps necessary to make it happen within a given period of time. Next I would plan, using my calendar, which business activities I would specifically do. I scheduled the actions on a weekly basis. When I planned activities and tracked them, my goal very often became a reality.

For example, if it's a financial goal for the month, you plan what activities should be done this month to achieve that cumulative result. At Creative Memories, that can mean deciding how many classes you need to teach each week, based on your average profit per class. You'll also want to plan what to do to build long-term financial gains. Setting short-term goals helps you to see progress. Having long-term goals helps you see the bigger picture and have long-term resolve to obtain larger objectives.

Like most direct sales companies, Creative Memories rewards building leaders in one's downline. I set a goal to help the people I had sponsored become leaders.

Prepare for Greater Success Than You Ever Imagined

Dramatic life changes can occur if we allow ourselves to dream, if we set goals, and if we're determined to do what we need to in order to make them a reality. Personally, I went from feeling that my life had few options, to knowing that the possibilities are unlimited. Because my business is home-based, I am able to successfully work a business I love and still have my family as my number one priority.

> What you get is a living, what you give is a life.
>
> —*Lillian Gish*

My life has been enriched in so many ways since I started my venture with Creative Memories: I have experienced tremendous personal growth, made friends throughout the country, and been afforded travel opportunities, for business and pleasure, that I otherwise would not have had.

When I did what I loved, the money followed, in time. Though I never dreamed it was possible, my income surpassed six figures this year, and it continues to grow. I know this is just the start, and that I have a lifetime of adventures to look forward to. To think that this amazing journey began with an innocent acknowledgment that I loved to plant tulips and make photo albums!

Your future is truly up to you. I urge you to trust yourself, your dreams, and the knowledge that lies within you. You, too, can find what you love to do, learn what you need to in order to grow, and make changes with excitement and confidence. Expect the best from yourself. Choose the best for yourself. You deserve to be all that you can be.

7 ACTION STEPS TO SUCCESS

1. Explore your passions to discover a business that is right for you.
2. Share your enthusiasm with others. Selling is a transfer of enthusiasm.
3. Keep going when obstacles occur. Persevere through disappointments.
4. Develop your confidence and your ability to communicate effectively.
5. Share what you've learned and empower others.
6. Set your goals and make an Action Plan to achieve them.
7. Prepare for greater success than you ever imagined!

About the Author

As a Creative Memories leader of a multimillion-dollar unit, **Nancy Smith**, of Chino Hills, California, has enriched the lives of thousands by sharing her enthusiasm for making scrapbook albums. She was inspired to begin her business because of her passion to do what she loved for a living. She's a top seller who truly enjoys exciting others about the possibilities that are open to them in a home-based business: the ability to work their own hours and to set their own goals, the opportunities for personal growth, and the income potential.

Nancy Smith, Executive Director
Creative Memories
3125 Skyview Ridge
Chino Hills, CA 91709
Phone: (909) 628-1072
E-mail: *CMNan@aol.com*

Creative Memories
3001 Clearwater Road
P.O. Box 1839
St. Cloud, MN 56302-1839
Phone: (800) 468-9335
Web site: *www.creativememories.com*

chapter sixteen

How to Sell More by Asking Simple Questions

PAM LONTOS
President, PR/PR

Have you ever started a sales call something like this: "Hi, I'm from XYZ Company. We have these products that . . ."? When you begin with this sort of opening, you have just sabotaged your own sale and set yourself up to be lied to—and you didn't find out if the client is even interested in what you have to offer.

Too many salespeople begin the sales process incorrectly. They see a client and talk immediately about their product or service and what they think the client needs. Successful salespeople know they can never assume they know their client's wants and needs. They realize that people buy for their reasons, not the salesperson's. In order to close the sale, you need to find out your client's reasons before you start selling.

The best way to learn what your clients want is by asking questions. Since the person asking the questions is the person in control, you need to ask questions at the very beginning and then listen intently to the answers. Clients will give you the precise information you need to sell them later.

The more clients talk, the more they think they are in control and safe. Talking helps them remove self-imposed barriers. When you ask questions, you establish a sharing atmosphere rather than a selling one. And when questions are correctly used, you don't make your clients feel as if they're being grilled; rather, they feel as if they are being taken care of by a friend or a consultant—a person who cares and who genuinely wants to solve their problems.

People Want You to Ask Questions

Ask the proper questions early in the sale, and you'll get a higher percentage of honest answers. When you haven't started to sell yet, your client's guard is down. Once you start selling, your clients encounter their fear of making a decision, so they postpone that decision by lying and giving you false objections.

A basic example of this concept is to ask early in the sale how much money your clients want to spend. People usually give you a figure close to the truth because they want you to stay within their price range. This doesn't mean you can't up-sell them by showing value, because they will often give you a somewhat lower price than what they can really afford. If you ask your clients this same question later in the sale, after you have started to sell them, they'll give no answer or an extremely low answer. By this point they realize you are going to sell them something and they clam up.

Another benefit of asking questions is that it lets people know you care about providing them with exactly what they need. They trust you more. Imagine that you made an appointment with a doctor because you were feeling

> You are what you are because of what went into your mind. You can change what you are by changing what goes into your mind.
>
> —*Zig Ziglar*

tired and sluggish all the time. No one asked you any questions when you called or when you went to the doctor's office. All they did was copy your insurance card. When the doctor came in to see you, he didn't ask any questions either. Instead he simply said, "I saw you were coming to see me today, so I decided to take out your appendix. See me Thursday at the hospital at six A.M. Here's the paperwork."

Do you take the papers and go to the hospital Thursday and allow him to take out your appendix? Absolutely not! Do you go back to that doctor again? No! Do you ever refer anyone to that doctor? Of course not! Did you believe anything he said? No!

> You don't sell them. You make them want it.
>
> —*Anonymous*

Why did this doctor anger you so much? Because he didn't ask you any questions about how you felt. Without questions, how could he know what you needed? Your clients feel the same way when you tell them they need your product or service before you ask them questions about their needs and problems.

Finding the Client's "Hot Button"

Salespeople need to use questions to unravel the secrets as to why clients aren't buying. They then need to use the answers they receive to learn what it will take to get their clients to buy. This is called finding the "hot button." The hot button is the end result of what the client wants. Only when you know the hot button can you sell the client.

By finding the hot button, you will know which way to slant your presentation and which product or service benefits will solve your client's problem. Eighty percent of your presentation should be geared toward the client's main buying motive or hot button. When you do this, the clients are easy to close because you have raised their desire high enough that they want to buy from you. You have found and filled their needs. Also, since 80 percent of sales is emotion, you must get them excited enough to make it easy to close the sale.

The hot button is the "end result" of what they want to happen, and appealing to it will cause this excitement. Most salespeople think they are finding the hot button when they find "needs." Needs are not exciting. Needs don't always motivate a person to buy. The hot button is emotional, and emotions sell.

What Does She Really Want?

The best example for understanding exactly what a hot button is and how it differs from wants and needs is illustrated in this health club example. Health club membership sales is a good example to use because the concept is so clear. After you completely understand it, you can write down the exact questions that fit your product or service.

Imagine that a woman wins a trip to Hawaii in a sales contest. She is so excited that she immediately goes to the department store to get a new bikini. However, after she finds a bikini in her favorite color and put it on, she looks in the mirror and sees her "fat, flabby thighs." No way does she want her friends and coworkers to see her fat, flabby thighs, so she rushes to the nearest health club.

Now, the salesperson at the health club is very health conscious, not weight conscious. He tells her that if she works out three times a week for three months, she will improve her cardiovascular system. Does this woman care about her cardiovascular system? No! She cares about her "fat, flabby thighs."

> Successful salespeople know they can never assume they know what their client wants and needs.
>
> —*Pam Lontos*

However, reducing her "fat, flabby thighs" isn't the hot button. That's a want. The difference between a want and a hot button is very subtle but important. Her hot button is looking great in Hawaii for her friends and coworkers. That's the end result of what she wants. Slimming her thighs is how she is going to achieve her hot button. Think about it. She's had those "fat, flabby thighs" for two years and did nothing about them. It was the trip and wanting to look good that made her come into the health club. Looking good in Hawaii is what will cause her to buy. Therefore, 80 percent of the sales presentation should be about how good she'll look to her coworkers in Hawaii in her new bathing suit. Sell to needs alone and you won't sell as much. Sell to the hot button and your clients will buy and say "thank you."

> Ask the proper questions early in the sale and you'll get a higher percentage of honest answers.
>
> **—Pam Lontos**

Learn What Really Matters

People buy because they want the end result of what they need. The best way I've heard this described is: "Don't sell drills; sell the perfect holes they create." Or, "Don't sell health club memberships; sell attractive bodies and more energy."

Think about these analogies: Don't sell cars; sell prestige and comfort. Don't sell insurance; sell security. Don't sell cosmetics; sell beauty. Don't sell computers; sell astounding reports (or awesome games).

You need to look at whatever you are selling and figure out exactly what the end result is that people want. An old sales adage says: "To sell Jane Brown what Jane Brown buys, you must see Jane Brown through Jane Brown's eyes."

Let's go back to the health club example of the woman going to Hawaii. She wanted to look good in her bathing suit. However, another client in the health club whose doctor has told him that he was at risk of a heart attack will have a hot button that involves improving his cardiovascular system. Likewise, the skinny guy wants to bulk up; the fat guy wants to lose weight. But then again, the skinny guy may be happy with his appearance and simply want more energy or to decrease his chance of a heart attack.

Which "Hot Button" Do You Push?

If what you are selling has many different hot buttons, how do you know which one you sell to? By asking questions and listening to the answers.

Let's take another example to show the difference between need, want, and a hot button. A lady with a painful back problem is told by her doctor to exercise in order to strengthen her back and stomach muscles. Her need is to strengthen her muscles. Her want is to get rid of her pain. Neither is her hot button. The hot button is the end result of getting rid of the pain—such as exercising more, dancing, even sleeping better. Exercise will also raise her metabolism so she loses weight, thereby gaining another hot button— a more attractive appearance. So if she's in your store talking to you about home exercise equipment, you don't just talk about strengthening the back muscles. You talk to her about the hot button you've uncovered with your questioning.

> Another benefit of asking questions is that it lets people know you care about providing them with exactly what they need.
>
> **—Pam Lontos**

But which hot button do you talk about? The one that's most important to your client. That's why you must ask the right questions. Her hot button may be getting a good night's sleep. Or she may want to ski again or dance. Once you find the main hot button, direct 80 percent of your sales to it. The real estate agent who just says, "Here's the dining room" and "Here's the kitchen" won't sell much. The agent who finds the hot button and applies 80 percent of her presentation to it will get more sales. There are different standard hot buttons for different industries. Here are some common examples:

Home sales:
- Location
- Large backyard for children and gardening
- Lots of windows and a beautiful view

- A unique design
- A school close by
- No school close by
- A large kitchen

Car sale:
- Prestige
- Safety
- Sex appeal
- Performance
- Economy

Clothing sales:
- Look thinner
- Sex appeal
- Comfort
- Durability
- Image

Vitamins sales:
- Health
- Energy
- Youth
- Recuperative power

You should write down all the benefits of your product or service, and then translate them into hot buttons. Then write questions that would ferret out these hot buttons. With every client, question them until you narrow it down to the one or two hot buttons that are important to them. When you find these, direct 80 percent of your presentation to them.

Raise Desire to Overcome Cost

People buy when their desire exceeds the cost. When they say "No" it means that the cost is higher than the desire. "Your price is too high" means desire is too low. Stressing the hot button over and over raises the client's desire. When desire is high enough so that it exceeds cost, then that person is easy to close.

Questions that will help you find the hot button are:

- What is important to you in _____ (a home, insurance, a car, etc.)?
- Why is it important?
- What did you use in the past?
- What did you like most about it?
- What did you like least about it?
- What are your goals?
- If it could be exactly as you wanted, what would it be?

> People buy because they want the end result of what they need.
>
> *—Pam Lontos*

Here's a good example of how complex and important hot buttons are. Imagine the cockpit of an airplane with all its controls and buttons. To someone who doesn't know how to fly, it's a confusing and frightening array. But to the experienced pilot, it's perfectly clear what each control does, and pushing the right ones at the right times is second nature.

Clients are like that control panel. They have an amazing array of buttons, and the salesperson's job is to learn how to find the right ones and push them at the right times. With practice this, too, becomes second nature. When you find the right hot buttons, you get the sale.

You Already Know All the Objections

After you've sold any product or service for one month, you've heard 99 percent of all the objections you are going to hear. It's insane not to have a way to deal effectively with every one of them. Otherwise, later when you close, the client will just use one objection after another to stall. If you let your clients bring the objection up themselves, you build a block between you and the sale. You either leave with no sale or you argue it away. If you argue, your clients will put up a bigger barrier to defend what they said. This will only make them harder to sell.

Objections are often our major stumbling block. We are going along fine in the sale until we hear: "I don't have the money," "I have to talk to my partner," or, "The price is too high."

Now we are at a dead end.

Do we "wimp out" or argue with the client? Neither, if we got rid of the objections before we started to sell! It may sound impossible, but it's actually easy when you sell with questions.

Preparation Is the Best Defense

Again, I'll use a health club example because it shows the concept so well. Later we'll apply it to other industries. When you go to close a health club membership, the client can put you off by saying:

- The location is wrong.
- I would rather join a gym close to where I work in a nearby town.
- I don't need it.
- I don't have the time.
- I'm not ready to join.
- I have to talk to my husband/wife.

To get rid of the "location" objection, you ask (during your needs analysis at the start of the sale) for more information:

> **SALESPERSON:** Did you choose this location because you live close or work close by?
>
> **CLIENT:** I live five minutes away. I can walk over.
>
> **SALESPERSON:** Great! Do you prefer a club you live close to or work close to?

CLIENT: I want a club I live close to.

SALESPERSON: Why is that?

CLIENT: Because I have to meet with clients in the afternoon, so I don't want to get sweaty working out. Besides that, I go straight home after work to have dinner with my family.

SALESPERSON: What do you want to accomplish at the club?

CLIENT: I need to lose a few inches around my middle and firm up my stomach.

SALESPERSON: What made you come in today?

CLIENT: I have a twenty-year class reunion in four months and my old girlfriend will be there. I don't want her to see this potbelly.

Bingo! No, the hot button isn't getting rid of the potbelly. It's looking good for his old girlfriend.

SALESPERSON: Do you have thirty minutes three times a week to look good to your girlfriend at your high school reunion?

CLIENT: You bet I do!

SALESPERSON: You realize if you had started a few months ago, you'd be in shape now.

CLIENT: Yes, I wish I had.

SALESPERSON: So, how soon do you want to get started?

CLIENT: Right away.

SALESPERSON: Now, when it comes to your own body, are you allowed to make your own decision?

CLIENT: Yes, I can.

What has this dialogue accomplished? Each of the main objections that could be used to put off making a decision was eliminated in this seemingly innocent conversation. When the salesperson closes, the client can't say the club is too far away, or that he wants to exercise near work, or that he doesn't have the time, or the desire, or that he has to talk with anyone else. Like a house of cards, all his potential objections come tumbling down. It is really beautiful to see this technique work.

> People buy when their desire exceeds the cost.
>
> —*Pam Lontos*

The salesperson never had to argue or apply any high-pressure tactics. People may lie when it comes to objections, but they don't want to look like liars. They remember what they have said and will try to stay consistent with it. Scripted sales pitches work very poorly in this type of selling. You are on a hunting trip and you never know where the client is going to take you. A script keeps you too rigid and tends to make the client rigid also.

What you say should be based on what the client just said. Even if you are trying to go east and the client just said "west," you have to figure out a way of saying "west" but going east.

For example, imagine you're a car salesperson who just asked the client why he's buying a new car. "The old one has been terrible and I'll be happy to get rid of it," he says. Do not respond, "Oh, well, you're going to love my cars. They are so reliable. Did you know that *Car & Driver* named this model the . . ."

No. Instead simply say, "Why is that?" Let him talk about what bothered him about the old car (this is going west for a while), then slip into telling him how your cars will never have any of those problems (going east).

> People don't buy from wimps.
>
> —*Pam Lontos*

A great way to prepare for nearly every objection is to write down the most common objections you get (usually eight to 10). Then figure out exactly what question would eliminate each of them up-front in your needs analysis. It is so easy to close the sale if the standard objections can't be used to stall making a decision. Let's look at some other industries and the questions you would ask to eliminate the objection:

Security system:
OBJECTION: "I can't afford it."
QUESTION: "What is it worth to you to install a security system?"

Computer:
OBJECTION: "I don't need a CD system."
QUESTION: "How could you use a CD system with your computer?"

Real estate:
OBJECTION: "This house overlooks the road."
QUESTION: "Would you prefer a home with an unobstructed view or one with another house right behind it?"

Insurance:
OBJECTION: "I can't afford it."
QUESTION: "What do you think it would cost you if someone in your family needed hospitalization for a month?"

Advertising:
OBJECTION: "You have low ratings."
QUESTION: "Do you want eight people in your store who have money and buy, or a hundred people who are broke?"

Office supply:

OBJECTION: "I don't have a credit card."

QUESTION: "If you bought today, would you use a company credit card or a personal card?"

Investments:

OBJECTION: "I'll think about it."

QUESTION: "If you like the investments I propose today, could you make a decision today?"

Furniture store:

OBJECTION: "Your price is too high."

QUESTION: "What's more important to you, price or quality?"

> Don't talk; ask.
>
> —*Pam Lontos*

The hour it may take you to figure out the questions to the main eight to 10 objections you get is nothing compared to the countless hours you would have spent not closing the sale. Remember, questions are your key to success. Ask the right questions in advance to make closing every sale a breeze.

4 ACTION STEPS TO SUCCESS

1. **Don't talk; ask.** If you're talking more than your client is, you're not selling. Ask your client appropriate questions to uncover their true needs and wants.
2. **Listen intently.** Your clients will tell you precisely what you need to know to sell them. The key is to listen to what your clients say and use their answers in your sales presentation.
3. **Learn your clients' "hot buttons."** Buying is an emotional decision, not a logical one. Your clients' hot buttons have to do with their emotional attachment to your product or service. Once you uncover your clients' hot buttons, sell to that emotion only.

4. **Prepare for the common objections.** Objections are your clients' way of stalling. When you know the objections ahead of time and prepare for them, you can turn them around into questions and get the "yes" answer you desire!

About the Author

Pam Lontos, MA, is a nationally recognized top sales trainer and motivational speaker. She is the former vice president of sales for Disney's Shamrock Broadcasting, where she is credited with raising sales 500 percent in one year. She is the author of *Don't Tell Me It's Impossible Until After I've Already Done It*, published by William Morrow. She is president of PR/PR, an international public relations firm that specializes in publicity for authors and speakers, and president of Lontos Sales & Motivation, Inc., in Orlando, Florida. In addition to her keynotes and seminars, Pam has many books, audiotapes, and videotapes available.

Pam Lontos, President
PR/PR
P.O. Box 617553
Orlando FL 32861-7553
Phone: (407) 299-6128
Fax: (407) 299-2166
E-mail: *Pam@PRPR.net*
Web site: *www.PRPR.com*

chapter seventeen

Putting the "WOW!" in Customer Service

MARY-ELLEN DRUMMOND
President, Polished Presentations International

Think about the interactions you've had with various businesses over the past year—your dealings with hotels, banks, airlines, stock brokerages, hair-stylist, doctor's office, car repair shop, grocery store, and coffee bar. How often did you find yourself feeling frustrated or upset about their customer service? I've put this question to thousands of people who've attended my keynote speeches and seminars, and have found that the overwhelming majority respond by nodding their heads as if to say "Often!" Here are a few examples of those negative experiences that they've shared with me.

I hate waiting on hold at my bank for a real person to answer the phone. One time I waited nearly twenty minutes to just ask them a simple question.

I can't stand the employees at _____ . You can tell they don't want to be there.

Sometimes _____ Airlines will give me an upgrade, and other times they won't. It just seems completely arbitrary.

Do I get these negative responses because most of us have only unpleasant experiences with people with whom we do business? Probably not. But the negatives loom larger and stick in our minds longer. Given this fact of human nature, we should recognize how critical it is that we deliver not just good, but "Wow!" service when we are the ones serving customers.

To get my audiences to focus on the kind of positive customer experience I'm encouraging them to create, I then ask them if any of the companies they have dealt with over the past year inspire them to say "Wow!" Listen to their comments:

I love how the employees at Home Depot don't just tell me where the halogen bulbs are, but lead me to the right aisle.

Everyone at the Wal-Mart store in my area is so friendly—they even have a greeter at the entrance to welcome you.

The person I remember most at Scripps Hospital is the wonderful nurse who was in the recovery room. She gave me a heated blanket after surgery, and she was so nice to me.

Whenever I hear these kinds of comments about "Wow!" experiences, I find that the situations have one thing in common: individual people making a difference.

By taking notice of companies and individuals who provide great service, and analyzing what they do right, we can develop our own "to-do" list for top-level customer service that will give us a competitive edge in today's crowded marketplace. Here's my "Wow!" to-do list:

- Lead by example
- Instill an "everyone is a customer" philosophy in employees
- Unlock potential with training and education
- Measure success
- Reward myself and others for doing well
- Exceed expectations
- Develop greater empathy and tact

You can cultivate these skills in yourself and your employees, using the guidelines that follow.

Treat Everyone Like Your Best Client

We never know where a relationship might lead. By consistently treating people well, no matter who they are, or what type of work they do, and whether or not they are already our customers, we cement relationships, gain respect, and build our reputation as a customer-focused individual or company.

> Study and learn from the best people and best companies. Consistently be your best.
>
> —*Mary-Ellen Drummond*

A number of years ago I was fortunate enough to be invited to a barbecue at the home of Glen Bell, the retired founder of Taco Bell. Despite having some 30 staff people there to serve guests, when we were introduced he asked me, "Is there anything I can get for you?" He maintained a gracious customer-service mentality. Because of his attitude I now automatically have a positive association with the Taco Bell brand.

Every contact we have, every phone call we receive, every transaction we have with other people helps build our reputation for customer service. For that reason, it's critical that we interact with our staff the way we'd like them, in turn, to treat our customers. By being respectful, polite, interested, and encouraging with our employees, we can cultivate in them a positive customer attitude, model the type of behavior we'd like them to use, and demonstrate the importance of consistency.

Inspire People by Leading the Charge

Before a seminar I delivered for a department of Disneyland Worldwide Service, Inc., I received a personal "behind-the-scenes" tour of the famous theme park. At one point during my tour, a teenage visitor toppled her drink. Without a moment of hesitation or a word of complaint, the upper-level manager guiding my tour began to sweep up the spilled ice and soft drink. The manager excused himself for a few minutes and personally went to get a replacement drink for the teen. I was impressed. He modeled exemplary behavior.

Even after most people would have retired, the famous Sam Walton, founder of Wal-Mart, was known to pick up trash in his stores' parking lots. Ray Kroc, of McDonald's fame, pulled weeds from the flower beds at his hamburger outlets. Successful executives know that first impressions count for customers and colleagues—and if they want their staff to willingly perform difficult chores, they have to be first to set the example and do so themselves.

> People are not changed by coercion or intimidation but by example.

Savvy management consultant and trainer Nancy Hancock Williams explains that "leading by example can be the single most important skill for managers."

Unlock Your "Wow!" Potential with Training

When I stand before God at the end of my life, I would hope that I would not have a single bit of talent left, and could say, "I used everything you gave me."

—ERMA BOMBECK

Although it would be wonderful if everyone knew how to communicate effectively and get along well with all types of people, the truth is that most employees cannot *instinctively* use the most tactful words, or exhibit the most persuasive gestures, or handle a customer's tense emotions. Therefore, if we want to provide "Wow!" customer service it makes the most sense to spend time teaching them how to do these things so that we can unlock the powerful potential that is there in our staffs.

> The expense of training isn't what it costs to train employees. It's what it costs not to train them.
>
> —*P. Wilber*

When we manage other people who deal with customers, it is especially important that we build training into the budget and one-on-one coaching into the weekly schedule. Once employees master the tools for being tactful, persuasive, and adept at handling difficult customers, they release powerful inner strength and can draw on their own intellect, expressiveness, and creativity in providing "Wow!" service.

According to Nancy Williams, a good rule of thumb is for a manager to meet with and coach each "direct report" on her staff, one-on-one, at least one hour per week. (If you spend too many hours per week doing this, you have too many direct reports. Seven or eight are about the maximum.) She also recommends a weekly group meeting to reinforce training concepts and share techniques for giving "Wow!"-level service.

Measure Your "Wow!" Quotient

Big companies have access to technology that can tell them in an instant how quickly calls are getting answered in their call centers, how satisfied their customers were last month, and how close they are to manufacturing 100 percent error-free products. But even if your company can't afford such technology, you can still set up systems for measuring your effectiveness at satisfying customers.

> Make it easy for clients and customers to complain. It isn't pleasant but at least you'll have the chance to keep the customer for a lifetime.
>
> —*Mary-Ellen Drummond*

Why should you go to the trouble of doing this? Because measuring gives you the opportunity to improve, and also the chance to celebrate improvement. The importance of measuring and tracking customer satisfaction struck home for me a number of years ago when I taught a seminar in customer service for the loan documentation specialists at a large national bank. In the morning session of their program I asked, "What percentage of your phone calls are from negative or rude people?" They estimated 90 to 100 percent. Later, I asked them to go back to their desks, track their calls, and let me know the true percentage. Amazingly, it turned out to be less than 10 percent. As I noted at the beginning of the chapter, negative experiences far outweigh the positive in most people's minds. Measuring shows us reality, and gives us a tool for motivating and encouraging ourselves and our employees.

Terra Waldron, a certified club manager and one of only a small percentage of female country club general managers in the United States, oversees a successful country club in Greensboro, North Carolina. She recently told me that the secret to her success is that "I know our members and our staff; I ask them questions. I am constantly finding out about their likes and dislikes, and learning how we can better meet their needs. Asking members and employees for their opinions not only gives you information, it also lets people know you care about them."

Celebrate Your "Wow!" Moments

Armed with our measurement data, we can then proceed to celebrate every improvement. You'll find that the more you recognize success, the more of it you'll get. For example, Mary Kay Ash, the cosmetics executive, is famous for the gifts, pink cars, vacations, and awards she lavishes on her consultants who work in the tough arena of direct sales.

One of my clients, the San Diego Convention Center Corporation, put on a Spirit Convention for their own hard-working employees. Employees got "served" with the same enthusiastic, professional skill with which they themselves usually performed. The convention team was inspired and re-energized by this special attention and recognition.

Hospitals across the country honor their staffs during "Nurse Recognition Month" or "Volunteer Appreciation Week." Many companies hold monthly award ceremonies and recognize employees for the attributes they want to cultivate as service providers, such as customer courtesy and responsiveness.

Rewards for top performance need not involve large sums of money, or even any money at all. Many employees thrive on having their strengths publicly recognized. In fact, one of the most potent management tools at our disposal is simple praise. When you approach someone, look directly into their eyes, and say, within earshot of other people, "You did a terrific job on this!" or "This is one of the best reports I've seen!" You will earn their respect, loyalty, and trust. As J. Marriott, Jr., once said, "We know that if we treat our employees correctly, they'll treat the customers right. And if customers are treated right, they'll come back."

> Make it a habit to praise people in front of others, and send at least one positive note each day. People need to be thanked and appreciated.
>
> —*Mary-Ellen Drummond*

Indirect praise can also be effective. A car dealership near San Diego, California, posts framed letters from happy customers all over their showroom walls. It undoubtedly lets employees know the standard they should aspire to and rewards employees mentioned in the letters. It also recognizes the customers who took the time to write.

Deliver More than 100 Percent

> *A sobering thought: What if, right at this very moment, I am living up to my full potential?*
>
> —JANE WAGNER

It goes without saying that we need to do what we say we will do. Credibility—the habit of keeping promises—is integral to customer loyalty. We have to push ourselves to deliver 100 percent. This may at times seem inhuman, but as Jeff Dewar, a researcher for the quality improvement firm QCI International, says, here's what would happen if some things were done right "only" 99.9 percent of the time:

- Every hour, 16,000 pieces of mail would be lost.
- In the next hour 18,322 pieces of mail would be mishandled.
- Every hour 22,000 checks would be deducted from the wrong bank accounts.
- Every hour 80,000 credit cards in circulation would turn out to have incorrect cardholder information on their magnetic strips.
- Every day two unsafe landings would occur in Chicago at O'Hare International.
- Each week 500 wrong surgical procedures would be performed.
- Each year 20,000 drug prescriptions would be filled incorrectly.

None of us wants to be the customer whose call doesn't get answered, or whose order doesn't get filled, or who has to put up with lost luggage, spoiled groceries, or incorrect prescriptions! So our goal in our own operations should be 100 percent. But to really stand out in the customer's mind, we need to go beyond simply filling our stated objectives. The most successful companies and people do more than simply ensure 100 percent service; they give themselves "Wow!" power by creating a brand image and going to extra lengths to maintain it.

> *When you're taking care of the customer, you can never do too much. And there is NO wrong way—if it comes from the heart.*
>
> —DEBBIE FIELDS, FOUNDER, MRS. FIELDS COOKIES

Nordstrom's employee handbook is a simple five-by-eight inch gray card that states, in part: "Rule #1: Use your good judgment in all situations. There will be no additional rules." This simple guideline has engendered the company's legendary service. My favorite Nordstrom tale came from one of my clients who had just purchased a suit. He admired the salesman's tie, and said, "What a fantastic tie! I should buy one to go with this new suit." The salesman agreed that the tie would look great with the suit, but found the last such tie had just been sold. Without hesitation, the sales clerk removed the tie he was wearing and gave it to the customer at no charge. My client was a bank vice president who went on to tell, and retell, the "Nordstrom tie story" to countless numbers of people. As professional speaker and author Jim Rohn says, "One customer, well taken care of, could be more valuable than $10,000 worth of advertising." Legendary service pays.

> Being able to hear what the consumer is saying is the foundation of our trends. And if the truth be known, it's the foundation of the future.
>
> —*Faith Popcorn,*
> The Popcorn Report

What gives us star "Wow!" power? Providing extra service and attention can sometimes seem like a chore, but the truth is that the little extras always mean so much—a follow-up call to see how a customer is faring with the new product, a note to thank them for their business, a small gift to acknowledge their importance, all help to let our customers know that we care.

From personal experience, I have discovered a great self-motivational tool: the "one thing more" philosophy. If I always do at least one thing more each day than I think I can, and one thing more than the customer expects, I can truly deliver exceptional service that will inspire a "Wow!"

> Being just average in business is a recipe for disaster
>
> —Mary-Ellen Drummond

Develop Your Expertise with Empathy

The Nordstrom salesman described earlier delivered "Wow!" service by putting himself in his customer's shoes. When we cultivate our ability to empathize, and see things from our customer's perspective, we can easily determine how to behave, because we simply do what we would like to have done for us.

Note that empathy isn't sympathy. Sympathy means you identify with the customer so strongly that your needs—or the needs of your business—become blurred. When we use empathy, we can see the problem from the customer's perspective, but we don't lose sight of our own. We can make a business decision that benefits us both.

Empathy involves active listening. Query the customer for more information, and repeat back to her what you've heard, so you can more easily defuse tense situations, clear the decks to solve problems, and gain additional insight into her needs. This can enable you to resolve the problem on the spot. When you do so, 95 percent of dissatisfied customers will do business with you again.

When hiring staff, I look for people who are naturally empathetic. I ask questions to determine if candidates are excited about learning, and able to change and be flexible. Do they ask questions? Do they lean forward, make eye contact, nod their head, and comment on what I said? Were they really listening? In hiring, we can take a tip from Disney: they look for individuals who smile a lot.

"Wow!" Them with Tact

Most professionals, including many of those directly involved in customer service, don't realize that the specific words we use, and the tone in which we utter them, can make or break a customer's attitude toward us. As advertising copywriters, poets, and other writers know, the impact of language is so powerful that even a slight change in phrasing can profoundly alter the meaning. Consider the differences in the following:

> Type this report.
> *Could you please type this report for me?*

> Please return this loan application by Monday.
> *Will Monday be a good day for you to return this application to us?*

> The product you want only comes in red.
> *The product you want comes in our unique tomato red.*

There is always a more tactful way of conveying any idea. I have found that a good way to develop increased tact is to write down the phrases and comments you make most frequently. Then rewrite them using words that are more positive and helpful. Finally, practice saying them until the new wording comes naturally.

"Wow!" Paves the Way to Customer Loyalty

If we genuinely want to achieve success, providing "Wow"-level service to our customers is the key to differentiating ourselves from the rest of the pack. Where customer service is concerned, we can't afford to have a "bad day." Research shows that customers who harbor resentments will leave as soon as a competitive alternative appears. Customers who are not only happy but thrilled with our service will likely remain loyal. It costs much more to find and sell a new customer than to retain an existing one. And very loyal customers are one of the most powerful marketing tools available to us. So go out and be the "Wow!" in someone's life today and every day!

11 Action Steps
to Customer Service Success

1. Closely observe the customer service you receive. When you get "Wow!" service, analyze what they did and add their techniques to your arsenal.

2. Remember that customers and potential customers are everywhere. Treat others as you wish to be treated. This includes your staff, who will model their behavior on yours.

3. Set an example for your employees by being the first to perform customer service chores. Demonstrate how to do it, and make it fun.

4. Provide training for yourself and your employees in customer service skills, particularly tact, persuasiveness, and handling emotional customer situations. Then practice, practice, practice.

5. No time to practice or coach? Make time. It is simply the most important thing you can do for you and your business.

6. Find a way to poll your customers and measure your results, even if you don't have a large budget.

7. Implement a plan for recognizing achievement, improvement, and success in your workplace. Emphasize compliments and praise, not merely monetary awards.

8. Do at least "one thing more" each day than you think you can, and one more than the customer expects.

9. Cultivate empathy in your "active listening," querying, and negotiating skills. Constantly put yourself in your customer's shoes to find a win–win solution for all problems.

10. Write down phrases you use frequently, and then rewrite them to be more tactful. Practice these at off moments—while driving, jogging, or getting dressed—until the new, more tactful words just roll off your tongue.

11. Consistently deliver "Wow" service and earn your customers' loyalty.

About the Author

Mary-Ellen Drummond, president of Polished Presentations International, is a full-time professional speaker, seminar leader, and consultant based in North San Diego County. She's the author of several books including *Fearless and Flawless Public Speaking*. Her programs emphasize the power of enhancing presentation skills, communication, customer service, and personal excellence. Mary-Ellen's clients include *Fortune* 500 companies, sales organizations, health care centers, and international associations. She has hosted her own radio talk show and is frequently interviewed by the media as she travels to more than 100 national and international engagements annually.

Mary-Ellen Drummond, President
Polished Presentations International
P.O. Box 2104
Rancho Santa Fe, CA 92067
Phone: (858) 756-4248 and (800) 728-9622
Fax: (858) 756-9621
E-mail: *medrummond@aol.com*
Web site: *www.medrummond.com*

chapter eighteen

Getting Along with Difficult People

FLORENCE LITTAUER, D.H.
President, CLASS Speakers, Inc.

Do you ever wake up in the morning and say to yourself, "I don't think I can stand another day in that office"? Then does your office staff come to mind, their idiosyncrasies lining up right there in the bedroom? Do you want to roll over and blot out that thought with dreams that end happily ever after, but you can't? First, there's Cathy Chats. No matter how early you have her come in, she's already had a day's worth of adventures to share. Her tale of driving through McDonald's for an Egg McMuffin could become a whole book, and you have to listen to it from beginning to end. She tells more than anyone needs to hear, and she embellishes her stories with such drama that the whole office stops work to listen.

Next, there's Bob Bossy. He isn't even the boss, but he sure seems to think he is, the way he offers his opinions on everything that goes on in the office. If he has one more suggestion on how you could run the place better, you're afraid you might scream and do something rash to his person. Careful . . . Cathy would sure make a story out of that.

> Every person on earth is born with a natural and basic desire that determines his or her future pattern or behavior.

You shudder when you think of Fannie File. She's the first person you see the minute you walk in the office door. Has she ever had a good day since you hired her as the receptionist? She always seems so depressed, and you're beginning to think she really doesn't like other people. Remember last week when she put her head on her desk and sobbed but she just wouldn't tell you why?

Then there's Larry Lazy. He's really the nicest person there, but he never gets anything done on time. He can make a simple job take all day, and when you give him detailed instructions he seems to draw a curtain across his mind and not hear a word. But, personality-wise, he's so much easier to deal with than the others. And you can always go talk to him and count on him to commiserate.

What can you do about this mixed-up group? Some days you even think, "If only I could get rid of all these people and start all over . . ." But you can't—and the next ones could be worse—so you might as well learn to accept them.

How to Get Along Productively

Getting along with coworkers is an increasingly important skill. In her book *Work Would Be Great If It Weren't for All the People: Making Office Politics Work for You*, author Ronda Lichtenberg says, "Everyone speaks from his or her own Agenda," and "Most people are defeated not by other people but by their reactions to other people."

For over 30 years I have been teaching about the four basic personality temperaments as they were originally written down more than 2,000 years ago by Hippocrates, the father of modern medicine. Year after year I've marveled at how the dynamics of clients' offices shift and evolve after they've put this invaluable system to work.

Identifying the Personality Types

How do you identify these different personality types, like Cathy, Bob, Fannie, and Larry? Using the following simple profiles that describe their strengths and weakness, you can pinpoint their personalities and identify where and how they will function best. You can't change them, but you can learn to accept them as they are and to keep them functioning in their strengths. From here on, you can put round pegs in round holes, square pegs in square ones.

The four personality temperaments originally were called the Sanguine, the Melancholic, the Choleric, and the Phlegmatic. As you begin to understand their profiles and see what each one needs to be productive and content, be ready to welcome a transformation in your office dynamic, as well as in the new, more positive way you face each work day.

Popular (Sanguine) Personality Profile

Let's do it the fun way.

- **Desire**: Have fun
- **Emotional needs**: Attention, affection, approval, acceptance
- **Key strengths**: Can talk about anything at any time and any place with or without information. Has a bubbling personality, optimism, sense of humor, storytelling ability, likes people
- **Key weaknesses**: Disorganized, can't remember details or names, exaggerates, not serious about anything, trusts others to do the work, too gullible and naïve

- **Get depressed when**: Life is no fun and no one seems to love them
- **Are afraid of**: Being unpopular or bored, having to live by the clock or keep a record of money spent
- **Like people who**: Listen and laugh, praise and approve
- **Dislike people who**: Criticize, don't respond to their humor, don't think they are cute
- **Are valuable in work**: For colorful creativity, optimism, light touch, cheering up others, entertaining
- **Could improve if**: They got organized, didn't talk so much, and learned to respect time
- **As leaders they**: Excite, persuade, and inspire others, exude charm and entertain, but are forgetful and poor on follow-through
- **Tend to marry**: Perfect Melancholics who are sensitive and serious, but the Populars quickly tire of having to cheer them up all the time, and of being made to feel inadequate and stupid
- **Reaction to stress**: Leave the scene, go shopping, find a fun group, create excuses, blame others

Powerful (Choleric) Personality Profile

Let's do it my way.

- **Desire**: Have control
- **Emotional needs**: Sense of obedience, appreciation for accomplishments, credit for their ability
- **Key strengths**: Can take charge of anything instantly, can make quick, correct judgments
- **Key weaknesses**: Too bossy, domineering, autocratic, insensitive, impatient, unwilling to delegate or give credit to others
- **Get depressed when**: Life is out of control and people won't do things their way

- **Are afraid of**: Losing control of anything, such as losing a job, not being promoted, becoming seriously ill, having a rebellious child or unsupportive mate
- **Like people who**: Are supportive and submissive, see things their way, cooperate quickly, and let them take credit
- **Dislike people who**: Are lazy and not interested in working constantly, who buck their authority, get independent, or aren't loyal
- **Are valuable in work**: Because they can accomplish more than anyone else in a shorter time and are usually right, but may stir up trouble
- **Could improve if**: They allowed others to make decisions, delegated authority, became more patient, didn't expect everyone to produce as they do
- **As leaders they**: Have a natural feel for being in charge, a quick sense of what will work, and a sincere belief in their ability to achieve, but may overwhelm less aggressive people
- **Tend to marry**: Peaceful Phlegmatics who will quietly obey and not buck their authority, but who never accomplish enough or get excited over their projects
- **Reaction to stress**: Tighten control, work harder, exercise more, get rid of offender

Perfect (Melancholic) Personality Profile

Let's do it the right way.

- **Desire**: Have it right
- **Emotional needs**: Sense of stability, space, silence, sensitivity, and support
- **Key strengths**: Organized, can set long-range goals, have high standards and ideals, analyze deeply

- **Key weaknesses**: Easily depressed, spend too much time on preparation, too focused on details, remember negatives, suspicious of others
- **Get depressed when**: Life is out of order, standards aren't met, no one seems to care
- **Are afraid of**: No one understanding how they really feel, making mistakes, having to compromise standards
- **Like people who**: Are serious, intellectual, deep, and can hold sensible conversation
- **Dislike people who**: Are lightweights, forgetful, late, disorganized, superficial, prevaricating, and unpredictable
- **Are valuable in work**: For sense of details, love of analysis, follow-through, high standards of performance, compassion for the hurting
- **Could improve if**: They didn't take life quite so seriously and didn't insist others be perfectionists, too
- **As leaders they**: Organize well, are sensitive to people's feelings, have deep creativity, want quality performance
- **Tend to marry**: Popular Sanguines for their personalities and social skills, but soon try to shut them up and get them on a schedule, becoming depressed when they don't respond
- **Reaction to stress**: Withdraw, get lost in a book, become depressed, give up, focus on the problems

Peaceful (Phlegmatic) Personality Profile

Let's do it the easy way.

- **Desire**: Have no conflict, keep peace
- **Emotional needs**: Sense of respect, feeling of worth, understanding, emotional support
- **Key strengths**: Balance, even disposition, dry sense of humor, pleasing personality

- **Key weaknesses**: Lack of decisiveness, enthusiasm, and energy; no obvious flaws, but a hidden will of iron
- **Get depressed when**: Life is full of conflict, they have to face a personal confrontation, no one wants to help, the buck stops with them
- **Are afraid of**: Having to deal with a major personal problem, being left holding the bag, making major changes
- **Like people who**: Will make decisions for them, will recognize their strengths, will not ignore them, will give them respect
- **Dislike people who**: Are too pushy, too loud, and expect too much of them
- **Are valuable in work**: Because they cooperate and are a calming influence, keep peace, mediate between contentious people, objectively solve problems
- **Could improve if**: They set goals and were self-motivated, they were willing to do more and move faster, and could face their own problems as well as they handle other peoples'
- **As leaders they**: Keep calm, cool, and collected; don't make impulsive decisions, are well liked and inoffensive, won't cause trouble, but don't often come up with brilliant new ideas
- **Tend to marry**: Powerful Cholerics because they respect their strength and decisiveness, but later the Peacefuls get tired of being pushed around and looked down upon
- **Reaction to stress**: Hide from it, watch television, eat, tune out of life

Recognizing the Four Personality Types

THE POPULAR PERSONALITY

The basic desire of the Popular Personality is to have fun. Cathy is like that. She would rather talk than work. She's really colorful and amusing as long as you remember she doesn't let the facts get in the way of a good story. She really likes you and desperately wants your attention and approval. If you'd listen attentively to *one* of her stories each day, tell her how much fun she is, and how much you appreciate her work, she'd stop trying to grab at you all day long.

Here's an example of what would work with our fictional Sanguine: "Great story, Cathy. You sure do have all the fun. We're lucky to have you on our team! When things get tense you sure know how to lighten us up. Now let's dig in!"

THE POWERFUL PERSONALITY

The basic desire of the Powerful Personality, like Bob Bossy, is to be in control. He is only happy when he is in charge of something. He has positive and creative business ideas, even though they aren't necessarily what you want to hear. He desperately wants you to listen to his suggestions and thank him for thinking of the good of the company. He derives his satisfaction from being a bottom-line person, and you tend to cut him off before he gets to that line. If you would praise him for his good work and let him know you are behind him, he would work harder and achieve even more.

An example of a good response to him is: "That's a great suggestion, Bob. Thanks for thinking of the business even on your off hours. I'll give some consideration to these ideas, and then we'll get back together. I don't know how you do so much in a given day." He will be thrilled you've noticed and will work even harder in hopes of more praise.

THE PERFECT PERSONALITY

Fannie File is the Perfect Personality whose basic desire is to have everything organized and in order. Her motto is "If it's worth doing, it's worth doing right." She is much better with numbers, charts, and details than with people—people drain her energy. So many of them don't do things right, and that gets her depressed. You are too blunt with her, as she needs sensitivity and your support. When she's upset, she won't tell you what it is about—then you get upset and leave her. She needs you to call her in when she seems emotional and ask her in a quiet voice what is bothering her.

When in private, she will tell you what's on her mind. Let her know you understand and will try to help the people involved be more sensitive to her needs.

An example of how to communicate with her would be: "You're a valued part of our team and I certainly want to be supportive. You're the only one who sees all the details that I tend to miss. Thank you for noticing them and pointing them out to me."

THE PEACEFUL PERSONALITY

The perfect example of the Peaceful Personality is Larry Lazy. These people try to avoid responsibility and all conflict. They are great listeners and have an objective opinion on everyone in the office. Larry is a good ear for you because he sits quietly and observes.

> I praise loudly, I blame softly.
>
> —*Catherine II*

He wants everyone to like him, so he agrees with both sides of every issue. This upsets you when you want a clear, quick answer, but his balance is an asset to your group. Larry is not self-motivated so you need to spell out clearly what you want done and give him time schedules for the finished product. When he misses deadlines, don't get emotionally upset with him, because anger and conflict will paralyze him, and he'll respond by doing less and less. Encourage him.

Here's an example of the kind of communication that will best motivate a Phlegmatic: "You are such an asset with your personality. Everyone likes you, and I need the balance and objectivity you bring to our office. Let's continue to support each other."

Working with the Four Personality Types

Everyone is born with a natural and basic desire that sets his or her pattern of behavior. If you know nothing beyond the fact that the Popular Personality judges all of life by whether each activity will provide fun, the Powerful Personality by whether they can get control of what's ahead, the Perfect Personality by whether each project can be done correctly to their high standards, and the Peaceful Personality by whether they can function without stress, conflict, or confrontation, you will be way ahead of most everyone else.

Now it's time to put your new understanding of the four personality temperaments to work. The following 10 steps contain what you need to know to get along with and to effectively manage the four personality types in your work situation.

Simple Steps

1. **Look at yourself.** Review your strengths and weaknesses to reveal your inborn personality. If you feel you have no weaknesses, realize that others may see you from a different perspective. Listen to the following inner dialogue and see if it matches your own. Be honest. "I don't think I'm impatient. If these dummies would only do what I tell them to do when I tell them to do it, I wouldn't get angry!" Does this sound like you? Guess which type you are . . .

2. **Look at others.** Realize that everyone is born with a personality they didn't ask for. Working with others' natures will always be better than trying to change them. Haven't you already tried remaking others and failed? They just don't get it . . . because they can't!

3. **Look for personality blends.** Although we are born with one dominant Personality we usually have a secondary one as well. A Powerful Choleric who likes to work can also be a Popular Sanguine who makes the job fun at the same time. A Perfect Melancholic in your office who is detail-oriented may also be a Peaceful Phlegmatic, taking his or her time to get things just right. Sometimes we "mask" by taking on the behavior of another Personality so that we fit in. A Peaceful Phlegmatic secretary may learn to be more assertive with clients on the telephone, but it is not her "nature" and does not come easily to her. Looking for more than one Personality in your coworkers will help you understand them even better.

4. **Learn to meet emotional needs.** Now that you know why Cathy Chats is desperate for your attention, Bob Bossy must be in charge of something and be praised for each accomplishment, Fannie File is depressed because she's dealing with imperfect people who exhaust her, and Larry Lazy needs schedules and deadlines to produce on time, why not deal with them according to their needs? Be willing to recognize that your old ways really didn't work.

5. **Learn to communicate on their level.** Part of meeting others' emotional needs is learning to "speak their language." Knowing this, you can begin to help people in your office communicate more effectively with one another. For example, you might suggest to Cathy Chats (Popular Sanguine) that she not use too much or inappropriate humor when she is communicating with Fannie File (Perfect Melancholic) because Fannie cannot give serious consideration to what Cathy has to say. Similarly, advise Bob Bossy to tone down his voice when he talks to Larry Lazy or Larry will shut down emotionally. Remember, with Peaceful Phlegmatics, tone down; with Perfect Melancholics, get serious; with cheerful Sanguines, lighten up; and with Powerful Cholerics, get to the bottom line!

> Blessed are the flexible, for they shall not be out of shape.
>
> —*Michael McGriff, M.D.*

6. **Learn to "staff your weaknesses."** Sometimes when we hire others we pick Personalities just like us. Here are some things to consider. Although we might feel more comfortable with another Phlegmatic, who's going to motivate us and keep us on track? By surrounding ourselves with those who have the natural strengths we lack, we all become much more effective. If you are not outgoing by nature, put Cathy Chats on your phone or place her at the front desk where she will be able to warmly greet your clients. If you're like Cathy—a bright, sparkly Sanguine and definitely not a

detail person—make sure you hire Fannie File as your personal manager so she can keep track of your appointments!

7. **Listen to their input.** Ask your employees or coworkers to tell you what they like and don't like about their jobs or the workplace, or what changes they would recommend. This can give you valuable insight and allow you to take advantage of the strengths of all the Personalities in your office. You will most likely be able to make some changes that will streamline your operation, increase customer satisfaction, and result in greater company profitability!

8. **Reorganize the positions.** If you have control over who works where, rethink the current placements with the personalities in mind. Wouldn't Cathy be better in Fannie's job greeting those who enter, using her conversational skills, answering the phone and planning the monthly office party? Or should she be out on the road selling, charming others into needing your products? Similarly, shouldn't you relieve Fannie of the emotional strain from dealing with those people who interrupt her work? Can you give her an office away from others, allowing her to double her productivity? Use her intelligence and love of details to their best effect instead of thwarting her progress each day. Could you give Bob projects that he can control and praise him when he completes assignments early? Can't you bring him in once a week and ask for suggestions? He might make you look better. Could you give Larry recognition for his faithfulness and balance, and tell him how valuable he is to you and the business? Realize he is not self-motivated like Bob and that you need to challenge him with lists, goals, and timelines. Follow up on his assignments and keep telling him of his personal value to you. Know that loud criticism paralyzes the Peaceful Personality.

> Do not withhold good from those who deserve it, when it is in your power to act.
>
> **—Proverbs 3:27**

9. **Encourage others to read this chapter.** Office workers can change their opinions of each other and accept those who are not like them quite quickly when they begin to see that "different isn't wrong." Discuss the personality temperaments with them and even suggest that they read the books *Personality Plus: How to Understand Others by Understanding Yourself* and *Personality Puzzle: Piecing Together the Personalities in Your Workplace* (Flemin H. Revell Co.).

> The next time some-one pushes your buttons, remind yourself that you're the one who installed them.
>
> —*C. Leslie Charles*

10. **Realize you don't need to be a psychiatrist to understand difficult people.** Some of us throw our hands up in the air in hopeless disgust at all those people we can't understand. From now on you should be able to spot the different personalities and realize they were born this way; they're not out to get you. You will know what it is you need to give each one to help them achieve success.

Starting tomorrow you can wake up with a positive attitude toward your "difficult people." You can be grateful that Cathy Chats will have a funny story to start your day, knowing that she will flourish in a position that requires talking to the people. You can be glad you have Bob Bossy because you can put him in control of a major project, relieving you of some of the burden you've been shouldering alone. You will have a new view of Fannie File once she's off by herself working perfectly and no longer depressed. You will still have Larry Lazy as a grounding rod who'll work with new zeal when he knows each day what you want him to accomplish.

10 STEPS TO GETTING ALONG WITH ALMOST ANYBODY

1. Learn the four basic personalities.
2. Study your own strengths and weaknesses.
3. Observe people for practice.
4. Know that the Popular Personality is the life of the party but doesn't like to get down to business.
5. Know that the Perfect Personality does everything right but may be critical of others.
6. Know that the Powerful Personality is the super-achiever but may offend others along the way.
7. Know that the Peaceful Personality is the easiest to get along with but may not accomplish much.
8. Meet others' emotional needs and reap the rewards.
9. Analyze the people you work with to see if they're in the right jobs.
10. "Staff your weaknesses" and find new joy in your job.

About the Author

Florence Littauer, D.H., is a prolific author and a personality expert. Her bestselling book *Personality Plus* has sold 1 million copies and has been translated into 23 languages. She is a seminar and keynote speaker as well as the president and founder of CLASS Speakers, Inc. The NSA (National Speakers Association) has designated Littauer as a Certified Speaking Professional and inducted her into the Speakers Hall of Fame, the two highest honors available for professional speakers. She graduated from the University of Massachusetts, has taught on both the high school and college levels, and received her Doctor of Humanities degree from Southwestern Adventist University in Texas. For information on her books or to contact her for speaking at your business, call 1-800-433-6633.

Florence Littauer, D.H.
President, CLASS Speakers, Inc.
P.O. Box 9931
Redlands, CA 92375
Phone: (760) 325-3661
Fax: (760) 325-1237
E-mail: *FredjLittle@aol.com*
Web site: *www.classervices.com*

chapter nineteen

The Challenge of Difference: How to Excel in an Increasingly Diverse Environment

SONDRA THIEDERMAN, PH.D.
President, Cross-Cultural Communications

Diversity is a funny thing. Some people like it. To them, being surrounded by people of different cultural, racial, and gender backgrounds is stimulating. These adventurous folks like nothing more than learning about a different way of life, eating "exotic" food, or being challenged by diverse expressions and communication styles. Others feel differently. More comfortable with people who are, at least in their imagination, "just like me," they struggle with fear and discomfort when confronted with someone whose life experience, point of view, or values are different from their own.

No matter how you feel about it, diversity is here to stay. More women, more minorities, more immigrants, more openly gay colleagues, clients, and customers are seen in the workplace than ever before. This increased diversity has a mixed effect on women's ability to succeed. On the one hand, there is a movement toward seeing to it that women have the opportunity to move up in organizations faster than ever. Yes, the playing field is, however slowly, being leveled. On the other hand, diversity creates a work environment in which things are more complicated. Each of us, no matter what our occupation, is faced with needing to modify our sales strategies, adjust our management style, and, more than anything else, stay alert to an environment in which behavior, needs, and values are no longer predictable.

> We may have come over on different ships, but we're all in the same boat now.
>
> —*Whitney Young Jr.*

A Look at the Challenges

Whether your work is in corporate real estate, pharmaceuticals, or your own small consulting business, your client and customer base is changing. For one thing, with more than 600,000 immigrants entering the nation every year, the chances of businesswomen encountering differing communication styles are very good. How, for instance, can you assess customer satisfaction if your customer is from a culture in which maintaining social harmony is a paramount value? For example, some Asian immigrants are apt to, when dissatisfied, say something like "It is OK" or "I guess I like it," rather than come straight out and admit how unhappy they are. We all know what a challenge it is to measure customer satisfaction—this becomes even more difficult in the face of differing ideas about appropriate communication style.

Your diverse employees, too, can create management issues that are new to previously homogeneous workplaces. The greater presence of women, for example, has increased the challenges managers are facing in dealing with sexual harassment issues. Similarly, there are more complex questions involving child care, maternity leave, and executive mobility.

Those of you who do not have customer contact and aren't in management positions are still apt to encounter diversity challenges in that your colleagues and teammates are becoming increasingly diverse. If women are to succeed, they need to learn to work with team members who have very diverse lifestyles, points of view, work styles, accents, and even English language fluency.

Looking at Differences: When Does Diversity Matter?

The first step in learning to function successfully with diverse customers, staff, and colleagues is to know when, and how, to acknowledge differences. This may seem obvious, but you would be surprised how often I hear people say, "There are no differences between how men and women work" or the equally short-sighted, "I never notice the color of a person's skin."

Why are people so afraid of noticing differences? I think because somewhere along the line—most likely at the time of the Civil Rights movement—Americans got the idea that to acknowledge the differences between people meant that we were assigning inferiority to one group or another. Nothing could be further from the truth. Differences are real. Some of them we like, some we don't, some need to be adjusted to make the workplace function successfully. Still other differences are the very reason that a diverse work force is so valuable.

> We must learn to live together as brothers or perish as fools.
>
> —*Martin Luther King Jr.*

To give you an idea of what I am talking about, let's examine an area that I once thought was very superficial, but that I now realize can matter a great deal when attempting to be successful in business—eye contact. Think about it for a minute. How long do mainstream Anglo-Americans maintain eye contact during a conversation before they look away? The answer is about three seconds. Take a moment to recall an incident in which you were working with someone from another culture.

Did you notice any differences in the amount of eye contact they maintained? What was your reaction to that difference?

Right about now you might be thinking, "This is silly—what does eye contact have to do with good business?" The answer: A great deal. Differences in eye contact can result in misunderstandings that can cost you quality employees and valued clients. If, for example, a job applicant is from a culture in which lack of eye contact is a sign of respect, but you misinterpret it as an indication of dishonesty, you are apt to dismiss that individual without fully investigating his or her qualifications.

It is beyond the scope of this article to go into detail about all the types of differences you might encounter. Suffice it to say that I learned long ago that to succeed in our increasingly diverse business environment, we need to stay alert to the possibility that those around us are different in some fundamental ways.

Understanding What We Share

Having said that, what about the other side of the coin? Yes, we differ, but human beings share a great deal more than most of us realize. Every culture, every person—regardless of personality, national origin, or sexual preference—values four things in life. First, everyone needs some degree of physical comfort. Second, we all require some type of security—a vague idea of where our next meal is coming from or the ability to believe that we will be reasonably sheltered from the elements. Everyone also has a need for social support—love, family, companionship. And, finally, everyone requires some form of dignity.

The tricky part is that each of these fundamental needs is satisfied differently for people from different backgrounds. If, for example, you are a manager, you can be assured that all your employees want some type of dignity. For most individualistic native-born Americans, this dignity may come from being named "employee of the month" and having attention drawn to them as individuals. For the group-oriented Vietnamese immigrant, on the other hand, many of whom value large group membership as a means of support, a more appropriate reward would be to give credit to the entire group for an achievement.

Are you confused? One minute it seems I'm saying we all want the same things, the next minute that we don't. How can you keep it straight? This is the easy part: Ask. Reach out to clients, colleagues, employees of different groups and find out what you share with them. Generally, what you uncover will be based on those four universal values. In addition, we also know that most people value children, most do not enjoy being embarrassed, and we all want financial security. Have conversations, you will be surprised

> A prejudice is a vagrant opinion without visible means of support.
>
> —*Ambrose Bierce*

what you will uncover and what you can use to build better relationships with those who, on the surface, appear to be very different from yourself.

Stereotyping: Your Greatest Danger

Everybody stereotypes. You may think you are the exception to the rule, but it is almost impossible to get through life without sometimes making assumptions about what another person is like. That is what stereotyping is: the tendency to have an inflexible belief about a particular category of people. Everybody does it, and it does not make you a bad person. It does not make you racist. It makes you someone who is trying to sort out a complex business and life environment.

The tendency to stereotype is universal—every culture, every race, every ethnic group does it. And we all learn stereotypes the same way. We learn them through the barrage of signals that come to us from family, the media, rumor, and, most potently, experience. That's where the problem lies—experience. Unfortunately, it is negative experience that stays with us the longest. The result is negative stereotypes about groups of people based on one bad experience. For example, you may have one client who is unreasonably demanding and makes you look bad to your boss. It is only human to try to avoid people like that in the future. Unfortunately, the only way you can identify "people like that" is by the group they belong to—hence the stereotype.

Maybe you have had an experience similar to the manager of a bank in Southern California. She had hired a member of a particular ethnic group who embezzled money from the branch. The manager nearly lost her job over the incident and to this day has difficulty objectively evaluating other applicants from that same community. Because of one bad experience, she thinks of the entire group as dishonest.

Of course, she knows she is wrong. She knows that there are thieves in every culture, age group, and gender. But, until she is able to learn to shove that stereotype aside, she is in danger of missing out on very valuable employees just because they remind her of the one who let her down. And that's the problem with stereotypes: they keep us from being able to see individuals for who they are. Sure, sometimes the content of a stereotype may actually apply to one person. After all, stereotypes came from somewhere—there are people who conform to them. Perhaps that, in fact, is the biggest danger. We see one person who conforms to the stereotype and we say to ourselves something like, "Aha! I knew they were that way . . . see, there's one over there."

> Just because we are equal, does not mean we are the same.
>
> —*Anonymous*

And, yes, there may be "one over there," but that does not mean that the "other one over there" shares the same characteristic.

How can you diffuse your stereotypical thinking? You may be surprised to learn that, once you practice these steps for a while, it becomes rather easy.

1. **Acquire as much knowledge of and exposure to diverse groups as you can.** Take the group you are a member of, for example. Let's assume you are a Latina who is close to the Hispanic community and obviously knows many other Hispanic women. If I were to ask you to name one characteristic, other than gender and heritage, that absolutely

applies to every Latina you know, you couldn't do it. If, however, you were to ask someone who does not know many Hispanic women and who has been exposed to common stereotypes, they might say that all Hispanic women are Catholic, have large families, and are subservient to their husbands. You, because you know so many different Latinas, know that description may apply to some, but not to all. The more we expose ourselves to diverse groups, the more individuals we know, the less we are apt to make inaccurate generalities.

2. **Become alert to the stereotypes that you have.** When you see someone with a particular skin color, eye shape, body stature, or gender, certain thoughts come into your mind. Maybe these are neutral thoughts and that is appropriate when all you know about someone is how they look. Likewise, maybe thoughts come when you see a particular last name on an application form, hear an accent, or learn that someone is gay. Again, perhaps these thoughts are neutral with no judgment attached to them. Perhaps, however, they are not.

   Most of us are nice people. I would even go so far as to say that most of us are not what you would call racist, sexist, or homophobic. But that does not free us of the temptation to lump people into boxes. Sometimes, by the way, those boxes are not particularly negative. The sound of a Chinese accent, for example, might lead you to assume the person is good at math. A black face might call up images of a great athlete, and when you learn a man is gay you might assume he will be able to help you redecorate your living room. These are not bad things—most of us would love to be good at math, sports, and design—but they still keep you from seeing the person for who they are. You are seeing this false characteristic, not the person himself.

3. **Get in the habit of shoving stereotypes aside.** As soon as that thought—that generality—enters your head, shove it aside long enough to see the person for who they are. Don't

kick yourself for the thought. Remember, stereotyping is nothing to be ashamed of. It is merely a mechanism by which we try to predict the unpredictable. Like any other nonproductive habit, the point is not to feel bad about it, but to control it.

This three-step process may seem simple, and it is. But it also works. Like any habit, it takes time to break the old one and install the new. You may never, by the way, stop thinking the thought—" "Gee, she's fat . . . I'll bet she's lazy," or "Oh boy, another male boss—I'm sure he'll be sexist just like the rest," or "Yikes, a 'generation X-er' . . . there goes the work ethic." But you can be alert to the fact that the thought is likely to be inaccurate and that it will block your view of the person for who they are, what they need, and how they can contribute to your organization.

Ethnocentrism: The Importance of Knowing Your Own Culture

Ethnocentrism is a fancy word for being "culturally self-centered." All human beings look at the world from inside their culture. That culture might be the culture of being a woman, of being gay, of being younger or older, of a particular race, ethnicity, or religion. As with most of what I have been talking about here, there is nothing intrinsically wrong with that. The problem arises when we allow the screen of our culture, our culturally conditioned values and beliefs, to distort how we interpret the needs and behaviors of others.

> We do not have to be twins to be brothers.
>
> *—Anonymous*

Let's revisit the simple example of eye contact. Assume you are from mainstream Anglo culture, a culture in which moderate eye contact is the norm. Assume, too, that you are selling to someone from a culture in which extremely direct eye contact is combined with a tendency to stand very close to the other person during conversation. If, according to your culture, these behaviors are routinely interpreted as aggressive, it is going to be very difficult for you to do what it takes to maintain a good relationship with this person.

The truth is that direct eye contact and a close stance are, in many Middle Eastern cultures, for example, considered necessary to good communication. The traditional American can't see it this way because our culture is distorting our view of the other person's true intent. A common metaphor for this process is the fish in a fishbowl. Surrounded by water and glass, the fish naturally looks to the outside world and see the objects in it distorted and bent. He is essentially seeing the world through a screen created by his own "culture" of water and glass. The only way he can learn what those objects really are like—how to interpret the direct eye contact—is to learn about the other culture and to learn about his own. He needs, as we do, to first become alert to the fact that his "culture" exists and then to compensate for it when trying to accurately interpret the outside world.

> So, let us not be blind to our differences—but let us also direct attention to our common interests and to the means by which those differences can be resolved. And, if we cannot end our differences, we can at least help make the nation safe for diversity.
>
> — *John F. Kennedy*

Learning one's own culture is harder than it seems. The reason is that culture is like the air we breathe. We take it for granted and come to feel that how we do things is just the human condition, the norm. To overcome this blindness to our own culture, follow these steps:

1. Expose yourself as much as possible to other cultures. This may mean taking an extra few minutes to have a conversation with a foreign-born colleague or attending a primarily black church in your neighborhood.
2. During these interactions, watch for the things that surprise you, confuse you, or make you uncomfortable. Make a mental note of those moments when you suddenly don't quite feel like you know what is going on or how to behave.

3.   After the encounter is over, examine those instances carefully. It is in those moments that the clues to your own culture lie. For example, if you experience confusion when someone from another culture does not come out with a definite "No" to a request, but you know instinctively that their answer is negative, you have learned that your culture values more direct responses. If you find that a potential client seems to be consulting with everyone in his family before making a decision about a purchase and you don't understand why, you have probably stumbled on your culture's propensity for individual decision making. If an immigrant employee irritates you when she insists on calling you by your last name as a sign of respect, not only have you learned something about her culture, but about your own as well: Americans tend to value flattened organizations and the informality of first names.

Learning your own culture is as important as learning the culture of others. Without the ability to understand your own perceptions, you will forever be blind to the true motives, needs, and behaviors of the diverse people around you.

Nobody ever said diversity was easy. It takes knowledge, awareness, and courage to make it work. However, once we overcome the barriers that differences unfortunately seem to impose upon us, not only will diversity work more effectively for us, but we will be in a better position to build more productive relationships with everyone we meet.

7 ACTION STEPS TO PERSONAL AND PROFESSIONAL SUCCESS

1. Ask about people's individual and different needs and perspectives.
2. Adjust to people's differences without compromising your principles.
3. Identify what you share with those around you, no matter how different they may seem.
4. Learn about people of different groups so you can see them as individuals.
5. Observe your own stereotypical reactions to others.
6. Shove stereotypes aside so you can see individuals for who they are.
7. Learn your own "culture" so you do not project it onto others and misinterpret their needs and behaviors.

About the Author

Sondra Thiederman, Ph.D., has 20 years of experience as a speaker, trainer, and author on the topics of workplace diversity and cross-cultural business. The goal of her work as president of Cross-Cultural Communications, a San Diego–based training firm, is to help professionals function more successfully in our increasingly diverse environment. Sondra's clients have ranged from such leading firms as Marriott Corporation, Century 21 Real Estate, and American Express, to notable organizations such as the Arthritis Foundation and the American Immigration Lawyers Association. Sondra has been featured in two diversity training videos and she is the author of three books on the topic of cultural diversity. The volumes are titled *Bridging Cultural Barriers for Corporate Success: How to Manage the Multicultural Work Force, Getting "Culture Smart"™: Ten Strategies for Making Diversity Work*, and *Profiting in America's Multicultural Marketplace: How to Do Business Across Cultural Lines*, which was named as one of the best business books of the year by *Library Journal*.

Sondra Thiederman, Ph.D.
President, Cross-Cultural Communications
4585 48th Street
San Diego, CA 92115
Phone: (619) 583-4478 or (800) 858-4478
Fax: (619) 583-0304
E-mail: *STPhd@thiederman.com*
Web site: *www.thiederman.com*

chapter twenty

Gaining Recognition in Your Field

MARY MARCDANTE
CEO, MaryMarcdante.com

When you end your day, how do you feel about yourself? Are you excited about who you are and what you're doing? Do you regularly acknowledge others for their contributions throughout the day? Do you feel valued by the people around you? Are you conscious of how much good there is in your life?

These questions have the ability to stir up many new ways of looking at and being with yourself. More important, the answers to these questions will determine how much recognition and appreciation you receive and give in your life.

In 1980, when I started my image consulting business, I knew in my heart of hearts that I had a great idea and was an expert in this newly emerging industry. I also knew that all the expertise in the world wouldn't do me a bit of good if people didn't know I existed. As my business evolved into a speaking and training company in personal development, I learned through trial and error that the key factor in my continuing professional success was to *gain recognition* in my field.

Be Excited about What You Do, and Share That Excitement with Others

I am convinced that my immediate success happened because of two strategies that I wasn't even aware were strategies until many years later. The first strategy I learned at a friend's wedding reception just after I'd started my business. *Be excited about what you do, and share that excitement with others.*

As I sat at dinner with a group of people I didn't know, the conversation led to what kind of work we did. I told them how excited I was about this new business I had started. Two of the people at my table were producers for the syndicated television show *PM Magazine*, who thought my business would make a great profile. The following Monday they called and arranged to tape me doing my work. One month later I was on the air. That show generated the most phone calls the station had ever received and I received more than 300 phone calls in the week following the show, for private and small-group consultations and speeches.

Thank People for Contributing to Your Life

The second strategy I learned from my mother, Grace. It has brought me more pleasure than anything else in my life, as well as a tremendous amount of support and business. *Thank people for contributing to your life.*

My mother sent me a thank-you note, or called me, after every visit we shared from the day I left college to the last months of her life. She would tell me how much she enjoyed my company. A simple verbal thank-you for an effort made to a thank-you note or gift expressing gratitude not only makes the other person feel appreciated, but also adds to your own sense of well-being.

Let's take a look at several ways to increase our abilities to generate excitement about who we are and what we do and to recognize and appreciate ourselves and others.

We All Need Acknowledgment— from Others *and* from Ourselves

Recognition is important whether you are starting your own business, looking for a new job, or have been employed by the same company for 25 years and are ready to retire. In 1899, William James, the father of modern psychology, said, "The deepest craving of the human spirit is to be appreciated." One hundred years later this still holds true. We all need acknowledgment from others and, perhaps most importantly, from ourselves.

Know What Motivates You and Others

Understanding what moves you to action is the key to generating excitement and knowing how to recognize and reward yourself and others.

Rank the following values from 1 to 17, with number 1 being most important to you.

_____ Artistic sensitivity: Appreciation of the fine arts, culture, beauty

_____ Competence: Being the best in some area

_____ Creativity: Self-expression, using your imagination and resourcefulness to create something

_____ Environment: Acting as a steward for the planet

_____ Gratitude: Appreciating and blessing life and all that you experience

_____ Health: Taking care of your body, staying well

_____ Independence: Doing things on your own, freedom to do as you believe

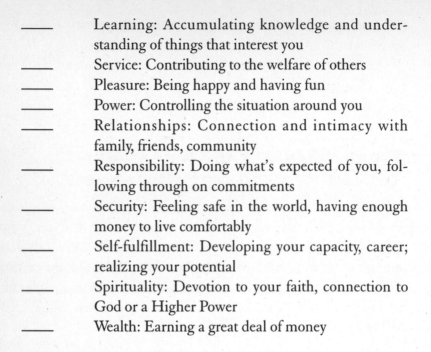

_____ Learning: Accumulating knowledge and understanding of things that interest you

_____ Service: Contributing to the welfare of others

_____ Pleasure: Being happy and having fun

_____ Power: Controlling the situation around you

_____ Relationships: Connection and intimacy with family, friends, community

_____ Responsibility: Doing what's expected of you, following through on commitments

_____ Security: Feeling safe in the world, having enough money to live comfortably

_____ Self-fulfillment: Developing your capacity, career; realizing your potential

_____ Spirituality: Devotion to your faith, connection to God or a Higher Power

_____ Wealth: Earning a great deal of money

Now identify your top five motivating values from this list. The next time you act in a way that deserves recognition, use your values as a way to reward yourself. For example, if you completed a difficult project at work, and wealth is important to you, ask for a raise or a bonus as a way to recognize and appreciate yourself. Or take $50 of your spending money and invest it in a share of stock.

As much as we hope for someone else to read our minds and know exactly what we need, it often doesn't happen, and we experience disappointment. Let the people who are important to you know what motivates you, how they can appreciate you, and ask what motivates them. You'll receive more of what you want in your life, and you'll feel more appreciative of yourself.

When you appreciate another, use their top values as a guide to reward them. If service is most important to you, but independence is most important to your coworker, instead of offering to help on their project, acknowledge their ability to get things done on their own and offer to be available.

Share What Motivates You with Others

Once you know your motivating values, then it's time to choose one of your top five values, get excited about it, and share it with others. If your top value is self-fulfillment, perhaps you've just been to a personal growth seminar that inspired you. Let your excitement show. If service is your top value, then spread the word about the volunteer work you're doing.

And remember to ask others, "What are you excited about these days?" In some cases, you'll get a blank stare, but I promise you that most people will think about and appreciate your question.

Acknowledge and Value Your Strengths

Right now, take out a sheet of paper and make a list of seven strengths, qualities, talents, and/or skills that you appreciate in yourself. If you have difficulty coming up with seven, ask others what your strengths are, or include qualities that you admire in others, and then work on developing and expressing those qualities in yourself.

Your goal is to be able to go into an interview and feel so confident when you're asked about your strengths that the words flow off the tip of your tongue. So read the list out loud to yourself every day until you have it memorized. "I, (your name), acknowledge and value my _____."

> Above all, challenge yourself. You may well surprise yourself at what strengths you have, what you can accomplish.
>
> —*Cecil M. Springer*

If you want to reinforce your strengths even more, ask a friend to read your list to you saying, "(Your name), I appreciate you for _____," and then respond after each strength with a "Thank you."

Learn How to Receive a Compliment

Too often I hear people put themselves down when another person compliments them. "I was just lucky." "It was nothing." "It was a team effort." All of these responses minimize you and invalidate the giver's appreciation. Alternatively, what many of us do when we receive a compliment or an acknowledgment is to deflect the recognition and call attention to our flaws or shortcomings. The next time a compliment comes your way, make it a point to stop and listen, instead of deflecting it. Let yourself take in the acknowledgment. Then notice what happens to your energy when you let the positive recognition and appreciation flow. Feel the lightness and breathe it in. That's where you will find your power.

There are three positive response levels to a compliment. The first is simply, "Thank you." (Not, "Oh no, that's not true; I made that all up.") The second level is, "Mary-Ellen, thank you for noticing," which brings her into the experience, and shows her that you value her. The third is "Mary-Ellen, thank you for noticing. Is there anything else?" This last statement was initially designed tongue-in-cheek, and brought a lot of laughter from the audiences in my Workplace Recognition programs. As people tried it, we all learned that asking for a compliment in a humorous way can sometimes bring more positive feedback. It can open the door to new awarenesses about what we're wanting and how much we're willing to ask for in our life.

Learn How to Give a Compliment

Researchers tell us that the leading cause of burnout, depression, and workplace dissatisfaction is lack of recognition and appreciation. In her book *The Worth Ethic*, Kate Ludeman comments that "when people receive approval, recognition, and praise, they become more cooperative and harder working."

Several years ago, when I was president of a volunteer organization, I paid a compliment to a colleague who had managed an extremely successful program we'd just completed. At the end of the day I stopped her and said, "Janet, thank you so much for all your help. You are wonderful." She smiled and walked away. I assumed she wasn't too impressed with my comment. Baffled, I caught up with her and said, "I'm curious. I'm getting the impression that you think I don't value the job you did. Is that what's going on?" She said, "Mary, you always tell me I'm wonderful. Next time, tell me *why* I'm wonderful." What an insight! People not only want to know you value them, they want to know *why* you value them.

Here are six tips to help you acknowledge others.

1. **Catch people in the act** of being themselves at their best, doing something good, honorable, kind, or helpful. Researchers at Blanchard Training and Development say it takes 12 positive comments to overcome one negative comment in the workplace.
2. **Be specific in what you're praising.** Instead of saying, "You did a great job today," say, "Thanks for turning that project in ahead of schedule. I was able to confirm the numbers and fax it to our client today."
3. **Use positive words.** When Peggy Noonan was writing speeches for President Ronald Reagan, she changed his words from "I'll never forget you," to "I'll always remember you." It may seem like a small detail, but changing your language from negative to positive can make a difference both in your energy level and in how people respond to you.
4. **Be immediate with your praise.** If you want to change your thoughts about another person from criticism to appreciation, you'll want to acknowledge a person's positive actions as quickly as possible. Do this for yourself, too. Give yourself praise throughout the day, and you'll be less dependent on others' praise to validate you.
5. **Be sincere.** Remember the time you flattered someone because you felt they needed to hear it and their response was one of surprise or denial. Perhaps it was because your intent was to make them feel better rather than to honestly acknowledge something positive you noticed. It is essential to tell the truth. Rather than flatter or patronize, acknowledge that the person seems a little down and ask, "How can I be of help to you?"

6. **Be personal**. Acknowledge how you feel about what someone else did. "Thank you so much for following up on that call. I feel so relieved that our client is pleased with the outcome."

Acknowledge at Least Three People Every Day

Take every opportunity to recognize others. Leave a voice mail, send an e-mail, handwrite a note and mail it. If the person is an extrovert, praise them in front of others. Fax a letter to her boss and the president of the company. Do something to express your gratitude to others. The more you develop your network of gratitude, the more your network will recognize you.

Create Personal and Professional Recognition Support Systems

> If you can't get a compliment in any other way, pay yourself one.
>
> —*Mark Twain*

Who are the people in your life who appreciate you? If you haven't told them recently how much you value them, please pick up the phone or write a short note right now. Tell them how important they are to you and what you appreciate about them. If there is one thing I can share with you about how to give yourself more joy and success, it's simply remembering to do this—appreciate people for what they've done for you and, more important, just for who they are.

Professional support systems will also generate more success for you and those you work with. One month after I did a Customer and Employee Appreciation program for a client, one of the managers called me and said, "Mary, we didn't believe it was possible, but we did what you suggested and it worked. Every Friday we get together and do a half-hour of appreciation in our staff meeting. Our meetings used to center around all the problems. Now people work out problems before coming to the meeting so they can get more appreciation time at the meeting." Imagine what our world would be like if we had more of these kinds of meetings going on!

Be Proactive: Turn Disappointment Around

In the best of all worlds, giving and receiving recognition would be a highly valued, common practice. Well, we're not there yet. As much as we might hope for others to read our minds and know exactly what we need, or to offer us recognition in any given moment, it often doesn't happen—even when it should, and we experience disappointment time and again. Is there any antidote to this kind of recurring disappointment? Indeed there is. It is to be proactive. Here are four concrete steps we can take to turn disappointment around.

LET PEOPLE KNOW WHAT YOU CAN DO

If you wait for people to notice your strengths, compliment you, and ask you to get involved, you could be waiting a long time. Rather than sitting back, passively waiting for others to invite you in, speak up and tell others what you can do. Whenever you introduce yourself to others, have a 15- to 20-second introduction that includes what you do, and start by describing yourself before you say your name. This will

> Good thoughts not delivered mean squat.
>
> —*Ken Blanchard*

help a person remember you more easily. "I am a professional speaker, trainer, and writer who helps people discover their best and make healthier choices. My name is Mary Marcdante. I'd be happy to contribute. Whom do I talk to?"

BE WILLING TO ACKNOWLEDGE YOURSELF IN FRONT OF OTHERS

In one of my communication seminars, Carol, the vice president of marketing for a software company, shared a phrase you'll want to memorize. She told of an in-house company meeting she attended

> Everyone needs to feel appreciated.
>
> —*Harvey MacKay*

where one of her peers, the vice president of information systems, brought up an idea for a new product that Carol had excitedly shared with him earlier in the day. Carol was flabbergasted that he never mentioned her name and was going to take sole credit for her idea. Keeping her cool, she said to him, with a smile in her voice, in front of the entire group, "Frank, I'm so glad you like my idea that I shared earlier this morning with you." Frank and the rest of the team got the message in a very nonthreatening way that Carol was the originator of the idea, and that she deserved the credit for it.

KEEP AN APPRECIATION JOURNAL

The Hawaiians have a philosophy that bodes well for all of us. "Bless everyone and everything that represents what you want." They believe that energy flows where attention goes and, by acknowledging what you're grateful for, you will bring more of it into your life.

Oprah Winfrey attributes the major successes of the past several years of her life to keeping a gratitude journal. This self-recognition of the goodness in your life empowers you as it reaffirms your sense of abundance and creativity. In addition, it is a permanent record of how much good there is in your life, which you can reread anytime.

ACKNOWLEDGE AND ACCEPT YOURSELF

In her autobiography, stage and screen actress Helen Hayes tells a story about meeting Mother Teresa. Hayes was fretting about what to say to her because she admired Mother Teresa so deeply for her humanitarian service. She felt her own work as an actress was unimportant by comparison. She decided to be very humble and simply say, "Mother Teresa, you do so much good." When Hayes was presented to the saintly woman, Mother Teresa put out her hand and, before Hayes could speak, said, "Helen, you do so much good."

You, too, can do so much good. Be willing to accept and recognize your greatness and share it with the world. We need you.

13 ACTION STEPS TO RECOGNITION AND APPRECIATION

1. Honor recognition and appreciation as ideals to strive toward every day.

2. Ask yourself at least once a day, "What can I do right now to better appreciate myself? What can I do right now to appreciate someone else?"

3. Practice regular acts of anonymous kindness every day. Help others with no expectation of anything in return.

4. Resist participating in negative gossip and move others toward words of praise and healing.

5. Have an opinion and express it. There are many situations and people in this world who need your voice and support.

6. Determine what values motivate you and others. Use these values as a tool to identify how to give praise and gifts to yourself and others.

7. Stop comparing yourself to everyone else and begin celebrating your uniqueness. Write down your top 20 strengths and review them daily.

8. Accept compliments with a simple "Thank you." Acknowledge, don't deflect, the gift of another's praise.

9. Offer honest, sincere praise or compliments lavishly and immediately. Don't wait. Stop by someone's office, leave a voice mail, send an e-mail, or even better, a handwritten note.

10. Give constructive feedback, rather than criticism. After telling a person what doesn't work, tell them what will work and direct them toward their future success.

11. Catch yourself (and others) when you (or they) have done something competently and give acknowledgment in the moment. Don't wait for others to do it for you.

12. Take a 10-minute gratitude walk outside every day. Give thanks for everything that your senses experience.

13. Keep a "Blessings Journal" and every evening record five things you're grateful for that day.

About the Author

Mary Marcdante is a dynamic and inspiring professional speaker, trainer, facilitator, and author. Her programs on appreciation and recognition, stress management, and communication help people discover their best, make healthier choices, and live their dreams. Mary is known for asking illuminating questions and helping people discover their own life-changing answers at conventions, conferences, business meetings, and school and community programs around the world. She is the author of *My Mother, My Friend: The Ten Most Important Things to Talk About with Your Mother* (Simon & Schuster/Fireside) and the postcard book *Inspiring Words for Inspiring People*. She is a contributing author to three *Chicken Soup for the Soul* books and writes regularly for client publications.

Mary Marcdante, CEO
MaryMarcdante.com
P.O. Box 2529
Del Mar, CA 92014
Phone: (858) 792-6786
Fax: (858) 792-4078
E-mail: *mary@marymarcdante.com*
Web site: *www.MaryMarcdante.com*

chapter twenty-one

The Spiritual Disciplines: Doorway to Character and Credibility

KAREN O'CONNOR
President, Karen O'Connor Communications

I had wanted to be a writer ever since fourth grade when my teacher, Sister Mary Pius, pinned my prize-winning story to the bulletin board in the back of the room one sunny April day. "This is a gold-star story," she said aloud, as she licked the small glittery sticker and placed it above the title line for all to see.

After school that day she called me to her desk, and in a tone that sounded serious to my little-girl ears, she said, "Karen, you're going to be a professional writer someday." Then her eyes sparkled like the star on my story. She leaned forward and a soft smile broke across her wrinkled face. "That star," she said, pointing in the direction of the bulletin board, "is just the first of *many* gold stars to come. Reach for those stars. Write the words God gives you."

During the early years of my career as a writer and speaker, Sister Mary Pius's words danced across many a cold dark night encouraging me when I was afraid, uplifting me when I was down, reminding me of my higher purpose when I had lost sight of it.

My first year in business I sold 12 magazine articles. I also received enough rejection slips to wallpaper my old fourth-grade classroom! It seemed to be a test of my resolve—and an opportunity to dig a little deeper. Would I give up or would I remain committed? Whenever the question arose in my mind I thought about Sister Mary Pius and my gold-star story.

I kept on writing, and the more I wrote the easier the words came and the more I had to say that was worthwhile. Sales to magazines led to books for children and adults, curriculum guides, and scripts for educational films. One film even won a Certificate of Screening at the Chicago International Film Festival. I tried it all— public relations and advertising copy, poetry, and fiction. I talked back to fear and kept on going.

Today, with more than 35 books published and hundreds of magazine pieces in print, as well as two decades of teaching and speaking behind me, I am humbled by the memory of that sweet sister who knew back then that none of what was to come would matter unless I wrote *the words God gave me*.

The Measure of True Success

Success cannot be measured only by the number of books we publish, speeches we give, students we enroll, customers we serve, or money we earn. *True success is about entrusting our lives and our situations to our higher power and doing what we believe we are called to do*. It's about getting ourselves right spiritually and emotionally so we can use the practical tools of our profession in a God-centered way. It's about aligning our character with the character of God.

The pressing need today is not for more women of independence—or for more intelligent, creative, or assertive women. The pressing need today is for women of spiritual substance—of credibility and character—women willing to make the inward journey to the deep treasures of the spirit.

Prayer and meditation, the life and breath of the spiritual life, is undoubtedly the means to that goal. A life without prayer is a life without power.

Richard Foster, author of *Celebration of Discipline,* says that prayer "brings us into the deepest and highest work of the human spirit. Real prayer is life creating and life changing." It is through prayer and meditation that we experience the quieting presence of God, commune with him, and receive his guidance. If we are committed to personal and professional growth, we'll be committed to prayer. Prayer is also the gateway to the spiritual disciplines—the paths by which we enter the life of the spirit.

Business owners and managers are beginning to see this truth as well, not only for themselves, but for their employees. Spirituality, once reserved for church or religious observances at home, is now finding its way into the workplace. Susan White, a professor of worship and spirituality at Texas Christian University in Fort Worth, says employers are now taking a holistic view of the spiritual needs of their employees.

> True success is about entrusting our lives and our situations to our higher power and doing what we believe we are called to do.
>
> —*Karen O'Connor*

At Leaman Container in Forth Worth, Texas, a small chapel is tucked between the executive offices and the plant floor. Owner Don Leaman says it's available for his employees to take a few moments out of their workday for prayer and meditation—if they choose. It's Leaman's way of showing his employees that he cares about them in more ways than simply how they perform on the job.

Gil Stricklin, founder of Marketplace Ministries, provides chaplain services to companies in 35 states. He adds a company to his client list every 10 days and he can't hire enough chaplains fast enough to handle all the requests. "More and more, employers are seeing spirituality in the workplace as a very positive thing," Stricklin says. "Life is tough, and when it knocks you down, you need someone to help you up."

Many businesswomen—trying to juggle home and marriage, business and personal goals—need that helping hand. Maybe you're one of them. I am. Sometimes we can't even imagine a life without struggle. But the very moment we declare our willingness to live in success instead of in struggle, we enter a process that leads to personal and professional satisfaction—regardless of the figures on the "bottom line."

What we carried alone for so long will now be God's. Think of it. God will close the old account and open a new one in partnership with you—a spiritual bank account that deals in the currency of seven spiritual disciplines: study, surrender, service, silence, simplicity, solvency, and serenity. Many of these disciplines are familiar. We have read about them, wrestled with them in our own lives, even practiced them from time to time. Some of us may have held back, assuming the disciplines are too challenging or time-consuming for women who must care for families, raise children, tend homes, and work in the marketplace. Or maybe you are one who has admired them from afar, assigning them to mystics and contemplatives who spend their lives in prayer and fasting. On the contrary, the disciplines of the spiritual life are God's gifts to every woman. In fact, it is on the ordinary streets of life that God does his most transforming work.

I believe that more than ever before, our world needs women who not only practice the disciplines but embrace them, not as an expression of legalism, but as an affirmation of a spirit who truly knows God as her source, her support, her very supply. The journey to the spirit is one that every woman must make if she is to realize her full power, presence, and potential in business and in life.

The Discipline of Study

One of the most important and often-neglected disciplines is *study*. Aspiring writers, speakers, and businesswomen eager to become successful frequently do not take the time necessary to *learn* the profession they wish to enter. Committed study—alone and with others—is crucial to growth and, ultimately, to success.

Find someone in your profession whom you admire. Speak with that person if you can. Ask for suggestions about what to read, what classes to attend, what groups to join. As a body of knowledge and perceptions takes root in your mind, it becomes the basis for your actions. It is up to each of us to choose, with care, the material we study and reflect on and the people we associate with who can inspire us onward in our search for fulfillment and professional success.

Objects of study might include reference books, anthologies on topics of interest, and biographies of professionals in your field of interest. You might also choose nonfiction that instructs, encourages, and provides practical application of a set of instructions or principles

> Real prayer is life creating and life changing.
>
> —*Richard Foster*

that will help you attain your goals in a satisfying and productive way.

This discipline also requires a willingness to make ourselves the object of our study, so that we might really see our own beliefs and boundaries, our patterns and prejudices. Without attending to ourselves both professionally and spiritually, we run the risk of continuing down the same paths while expecting different results.

Ultimately, the discipline of study involves a deep conviction and commitment to personal and spiritual renewal.

The Discipline of Surrender

No amount of internal satisfaction can occur in our lives if we do not give control to a power greater than we are. And yet no discipline has been more abused by individuals, families, school, and religious leaders. Surrender has earned a bad reputation. In some circles, it suggests a form of bondage, a giving away of all that is valuable and dear and unique to us as individuals.

And no wonder. Many women have been forced to surrender, made to submit, humiliated into subordination as children, wives, employees, even friends.

The discipline of surrender, however, has nothing to do with bondage. It is an expression of freedom. Giving up means turning over to God, for his safekeeping, those people and situations we have no control over anyway. Surrender releases us from carrying the process as well as the results. We can then walk in freedom, knowing with absolute certainty that the God of the universe, the one who knows all things, who is for all time, will bring about in our lives what is right and good and pure and just, not only in the professional realm, but in every area of our lives.

If our first act of surrender each day is to the God of our understanding, then we can proceed, confident that he will direct us to the places and people he has planned for us to serve.

The Discipline of Service

Some women may see service as the *doormat discipline* because they have, for so long, allowed others to wipe their shoes on them. But true service is far from that. Service that springs from the heart and soul is a gift of self. One who serves from the spirit knows when to say yes and when to say no. She knows what part is hers and what part belongs to another because she lives with one eye and ear attuned to the natural realm and one eye and ear fixed on the spiritual, the source of guidance.

I remember a time in my life when I had become dangerously out of balance. I was on a merry-go-round of self-abuse and didn't even realize it until I slipped into a depression that lasted several months. Then by divine appointment I was invited to teach a writing course as part of the Sierra Writing Camp. Little did I know at the time that I would experience a deep healing of my wounded spirit during that week. A conversation with two strangers led me to realize that I had lost sight of my true purpose—*to write and speak the words God had given me*. Instead, I had been trying to score points with God, please others, and make myself look good! My career and my personal life were transformed that week, and I've been at peace ever since.

The Discipline of Silence

My husband taught me a valuable and much-needed lesson about silence some years ago when he was caught in a desperate time in his professional life. We were newly married then and for a short stint he was forced to drive a delivery truck for a local cleaners. It was the only work readily available—quite a switch from his previous years in corporate life.

One of his favorite aspects of the job was the silence and solitude it offered. Each lunch hour he parked on a hill in his territory that overlooked the Pacific Ocean. "I look forward to that time alone," he often said over dinner at night. "It's *my* time. No one but God knows where I am. I relax, enjoy my food, read, pray, even snooze! Everyone *deserves* such an experience." His words made a profound impact on my life. "Everyone deserves such an experience." Words he might never have said, an experience he might never have had, if he had remained in his pristine office atop a New York skyscraper.

Charles drove up and down the hills of La Jolla, California, delivering dry cleaning for more than a year—at a salary that barely covered his essentials. Yet he felt incredibly successful because the job provided time to be silent and still so he could get to know himself and the God of his understanding.

> The world cannot always understand one's profession of faith, but it can understand service.
>
> —*Ian Maclaren*

For many of us silence is a fearful thing, an intruder. Perhaps as a little girl you were punished with the silent treatment by a disappointed parent. Or if you came from a large, noisy household, you may have longed for a few moments of silence but never got them. Or perhaps you craved a bit of solitude under a tree, or by a riverbank, or in a secret hideaway, where you could think and dream, or listen to the birds, or write in a journal.

As an adult it may be painful for you even to consider carving out a time of silence. You may not know what to do with it or how to benefit from it. The moment you sit down with yourself and your thoughts, you suddenly remember a letter you need to type, a blouse that needs pressing, a stack of papers that need your attention, a pile of bills that should be paid.

Silence is not an easy discipline to embrace. We talk about it, think of it, and wish for it, but rarely do we experience it. Entering silence requires a step of faith, a commitment to nurture ourselves, a willingness to stop the noise and see what's on the other side. It also requires that we practice being alone, moving into a space of solitude where we can listen and hear and experience the comfort and power of God within us.

Wisely, the writer of Ecclesiastes says there is "a time to be silent and a time to speak." Those of us who wish to practice the discipline of silence will heed those words.

The Discipline of Simplicity

What a great gust of cleansing wind we would feel in our lives and in our homes and workplaces if we surrendered to simplicity. Embracing this elusive discipline, however, involves trust and prudence—two virtues that are easier talked about than practiced.

Simplicity is not austerity. It does not renounce the things of the world, but instead, puts them into proper perspective. We trust ourselves to be well, look well, feel well, and do well—without making a "statement" or show of it. Our choices and decisions come out of prudence, not peer pressure or the need for others' approval.

A simpler life—one that is free of baggage, bulging calendars, demanding people, and unrealistic expectations—can be challenging to come by. But when we commit to simplifying our lives, to clearing out the clutter—from old files to old clients and acquaintances who no longer nourish us—oh, the freedom and the strength we feel!

A simpler life includes learning how to make wise choices about our clothing and transportation and office needs. Do we really need 25 pairs of shoes? Can we purchase good-quality classic clothing that will hold up for two or three seasons, rather than answering the call of every fashion trend that comes along? Are we willing to run our business from a modest dwelling that is afford-able and comfortable, rather than a showplace that drains our earn-ings and energy each month?

Simplicity also encourages us to modify our diets, to embrace simple nourishing foods that we can prepare at home or at work, instead of cramming fast foods into our mouths while we drive, or read the paper, or finish a report at work.

Simplicity, like all disciplines, begins on the inside. When we are simple within, we are free without. We can say "No" without feeling guilty, refuel ourselves with a good night's rest after a day's work, and consider our choices ahead of time so we don't over-commit, risking irritability, illness, and ill tempered decisions. Sim-plicity is the discipline that brings us down to where we ought to be so we can be lifted up by the strength of God when we need it most.

> Simplicity is the mark of a master-hand.
>
> —*Elsie De Wolfe*

The Discipline of Solvency

The discipline of solvency challenges us to discover our needs and wants, and to bring them into perspective and balance in terms of what is real and true in our lives—such as earnings, the season of our lives, the status of our businesses and households and dependent family members. Then, we bring all this before God for his guidance.

I have found solvency and simplicity to be closely connected. Simplicity provides a solid foundation on which solvency can be practiced. Solvency, too, is an *inside job*. What occurs in the spiritual realm will show up in the natural realm as soon as a woman com-mits to living her life free of debt and the emotional bondage of trying to keep up with competitors. Such women earn, save, share, spend, and invest out of a deep conviction, based on God's guid-ance, of what is right and true and just.

Practicing solvency in our lives also includes a willingness to learn all we can about practical financial matters that affect our everyday affairs. It means we take an interest in managing checking accounts, handling cash in responsible ways, planning for future needs and wants, setting aside funds for emergencies, investments, vacations, and retirement.

It includes praying for guidance about whom to talk to, which seminars to attend, what books to read and tapes to listen to. The discipline of solvency is the working out of an inward commitment to become good stewards of the resources God provides. A solvent lifestyle results in a deep peace that paves the way for a life of serenity—and true success.

The Discipline of Serenity

Serenity is a state of calm, of peace, of deep inner knowledge that all is well—*despite what is sometimes overwhelming evidence to the contrary*. One professional speaker I met disclosed that her husband had suffered a debilitating stroke, leaving him partially paralyzed and blind. Yet she was filled with peace and poise—speaking sincerely about the grace God gives her daily to cope with this unexpected turn in their lives.

A woman who started a business in San Diego with money from a family trust was making great headway when one of her employees embezzled a significant amount of money that resulted in the owner closing down. At first she was devastated, of course, but when we spoke she said she knew her higher power would guide her to the next decision. "I can be set back," she said with confidence, "but I can't be stopped—unless I say so!"

As a woman comes to rest in the God she knows and understands, she begins to accept what is. She holds life, herself, and other people with an open hand instead of a clenched fist! Serenity is the foundation for living a life of authenticity and credibility.

I cannot think of a better way to practice serenity than to live the words of the Serenity Prayer:

God, grant me the serenity to accept the things I cannot change, courage to change the things I can, and wisdom to know the difference.

Women who abide by these words no longer lean on themselves or the things of the world. They know their personal power is limited and they are effective only to the extent that God empowers them. They do not waste time trying to figure out what to do, what to say, or how to respond. They go to God *first*. And they ask for the power they need to accept what they cannot change. Then they ask for the courage to change what they can. This takes some doing—because it implies they will be given that knowledge, and they must then *apply* it.

Finally, and most important, they seek the wisdom they need to know the difference between the two. Without wisdom, their serenity would be jeopardized. In all cases, they come before God, leaning on his power and understanding, not on their own. And in so doing they release the results to God, further ensuring their serenity and the right and just outworking of God in their own lives and in the lives of others. What freedom!

> It is the muteness of the lips when the spirit speaks loudest.
>
> *—Madeline Mason-Manheim*

As we take up the spiritual journey to our center, we can turn to the spiritual disciplines, like streams in a desert, to refresh our spirits when we feel dry and to guide us when we are lost. And for those times when we are strong and sure-footed, the disciplines enable us to explore new terrain with the confidence that God, our higher power, is with us every step of the way—in business and in life.

Could any amount of success be more *incredible* than that?

7 ACTION STEPS TO SUCCESS

1. Choose with care the material you study, consider, and act upon.
2. Surrender your goals and results to your higher power for direction and safekeeping.
3. Remember that true service is self-giving, not self-serving.
4. Select small pockets of time each day for silent reflection.
5. Embrace a simple lifestyle so you can focus on what really matters.
6. Commit yourself to solvency by using your resources in a respectful and responsible way.
7. Experience lasting serenity as you release what you cannot control and govern wisely what is yours to manage.

About the Author

Karen O'Connor, award-winning author, speaker, and writing consultant, is a full-time professional in San Diego, California. She's the author of more than 40 books on a variety of topics, including *The Blessing Basket: 31 Days to a More Grateful Heart*, published by Water Brook Press, a division of Random House, and *A Woman's Place Is in the Mall—and Other Lies* published by Thomas Nelson. All of Karen's books and presentations are created with one purpose in mind: to encourage people to develop more intimacy with God, self, and others. O'Connor has been a guest on numerous radio and television programs across the United States, including the *700 Club, Coast-to-Coast, Life-Style* magazine, and the *Sally Jessy Raphael Show*.

Karen O'Connor
Karen O'Connor Communications
2050 Pacific Beach Drive, #205
San Diego, CA 92109
Phone: (858) 483-3184
Fax: (858) 483-0427
E-mail: *karen@karenoconnor.com*
Web site: *www.karenoconnor.com*

Index